THE LOCATION OF SERVICE TOWNS

An Approach to the Analysis of Central Place Systems

UNIVERSITY OF TORONTO DEPARTMENT
OF GEOGRAPHY RESEARCH PUBLICATIONS

1. The Hydrologic Cycle and the Wisdom of God: A Theme in Geoteleology
   by Yi-Fu Tuan

2. Residential Water Demand and Economic Development by Terence R. Lee

3. The Location of Service Towns by John U. Marshall

THE LOCATION OF SERVICE TOWNS

An Approach to the Analysis of Central Place Systems

JOHN URQUHART MARSHALL
York University, Toronto

Published for the University of Toronto
Department of Geography
by the University of Toronto Press

© University of Toronto Department of Geography
Published by University of Toronto Press, 1969

Printed in Canada

SBN 8020-3253-2

Acknowledgments

I wish to express my thanks to Jacob Spelt, Professor of Geography at the University of Toronto, under whose guidance I completed the dissertation on which this monograph is based. While my research was in progress, valuable comments were also received from Professors Leslie Curry and Alan Baker, both of the Department of Geography, University of Toronto, and from Professor G. William Skinner of the Department of Anthropology, Stanford University. In preparing the manuscript for publication, I received useful editorial suggestions from Professors Ian Burton, Larry Bourne, and James Simmons, all of the Department of Geography, University of Toronto. I also wish to acknowledge the influence of John Borchert, Professor of Geography at the University of Minnesota, who first aroused my interest in central place patterns.

The field work for this study was made possible by a grant from the Canadian Council on Urban and Regional Research, and a major contribution toward cost of publication was made by the Publications Committee of the Canadian Association of Geographers. I am most grateful for this support. Thanks must also be expressed to the numerous persons in the study area who allowed themselves to be interviewed, and who supplied me with much vital information.

Finally, with the deepest gratitude, I acknowledge the help of my wife, Gloria, who not only assisted with the drafting of the illustrations, but also provided the constant encouragement so essential to the completion of the work.

John U. Marshall
York University, Toronto
August, 1969

Contents

ACKNOWLEDGMENTS   v

TABLES   viii

ILLUSTRATIONS   x

I   INTRODUCTION   3

II CHRISTALLER'S THEORY AND THE CRITERIA OF
    HIERARCHICAL STRUCTURING   11

III HIERARCHICAL CLASSIFICATIONS OF TOWNS: A
    SURVEY OF PAST RESEARCH   44

IV THE DESIGN OF EMPIRICAL STUDIES   68

V   THE BARRIE AND OWEN SOUND SYSTEMS:
    LOCATIONAL ANALYSIS   109

VI COMPARISONS AND CONCLUSIONS   151

    BIBLIOGRAPHY   175

Tables

Table

1. Central Functions in a Hypothetical Central Place System   87

2. Centrality in the System Shown in Table 1   87

3. Patterns of Occurrence of Three Functions in a Hypothetical Central Place System   99

4. Central Functions in the Study Area   125

5. Barrie System: Location Coefficients of Central Functions   129

6. Owen Sound System: Location Coefficients of Central Functions   131

7. Barrie System: Functional Indices and Related Data   133

8. Owen Sound System: Functional Indices and Related Data   135

9. Barrie System: Hierarchical Classification of Centres   142

10. Owen Sound System: Hierarchical Classification of Centres   143

11. Barrie System: Functional Indices Adjusted for Manufacturing   146

Table

12. Owen Sound System: Functional Indices Adjusted
for Manufacturing   147

13. Barrie System: Incremental Functions in Successive Ranks   154

14. Owen Sound System: Incremental Functions in
Successive Ranks   155

15. Distribution of Centrality by Ranks   158

16. Population Thresholds of Functions   159

17. Continuous Functional Relationships   163

18. The Relationship between Population and Number
of Functions in Different Areas   168

Illustrations

Figure

1. Ideal Arrangement of Suppliers with Circular
   Market Areas   14

2. The Location of Excess Profits   17

3. The Viability of Interstitial Locations   17

4. The Arrangement of A and B Centres with
   Hexagonal Market Areas   19

5. Christaller's Versorgungsprinzip Model   21

6. Location of B Centres on Routes Connecting
   A Centres   30

7. Christaller's Verkehrsprinzip Model   30

8. A Model Satisfying Christaller's Absonderungsprinzip Conditions   32

9. Distribution of A Centres on an Anisotropic
   Plain   35

10. Classification of Central Places in Part of
    Iowa (after Berry)   57

11. A System of Central Places   76

12. Location of Study Area   110

13. Employees in Manufacturing   110

Figure

14. The Niagara Escarpment 112

15. Density of Unincorporated Population 114

16. Barrie System: Centres Classed by Type 116

17. Owen Sound System: Centres Classed by Type 117

18. Barrie System: The Three Highest Ranking Centres 137

19. Owen Sound System: The Eight Highest Ranking Centres 137

20. The Basic Lattice of Locally Dominant Centres 139

21. Interstitial Villages within the Basic Urban Lattice 139

22. Hierarchical Classification of Centres 144

23. Barrie and Owen Sound Systems Combined: Centres Ranked by Number of Functions 153

24. Barrie System: Relationship between Population and Number of Functions 164

25. Owen Sound System: Relationship between Population and Number of Functions 164

26. Barrie System: Relationship between Numbers of Functions and Establishments 165

27. Owen Sound System: Relationship between Numbers of Functions and Establishments 165

28. Barrie System: Relationship between Number of Functions and Functional Index 166

29. Owen Sound System: Relationship between Number of Functions and Functional Index 166

30. Barrie and Owen Sound Systems Combined: Relationship between Population and Number of Functions 167

31. Barrie and Owen Sound Systems Combined: Relationship between Numbers of Functions and Establishments 167

THE LOCATION OF SERVICE TOWNS

An Approach to the Analysis of Central Place Systems

I
Introduction

"Cities do not grow of themselves. Countrysides set them up to do tasks that must be performed in central places."[1] In these few words, Mark Jefferson summarized a relationship which has become the focus of interest of a major branch of urban geography. Jefferson himself did not develop the field of central place research, but he did draw attention to the servicing of rural population as an important factor in urban growth. Moreover, he may be credited with being the first to refer to a town's role in servicing rural folk as its "central place" function, since he used this term two years before the appearance of Walter Christaller's Die zentralen Orte in Süddeutschland, and a full decade before Edward Ullman introduced Christaller's work to the English language literature.[2]

THE CONCEPTUAL BASIS OF CENTRAL PLACE RESEARCH

The concept of central place may be clarified by a consideration of the basic-nonbasic interpretation of urban functions. The goods produced within any circumscribed area—in this case, an

---

[1] Mark Jefferson, "Distribution of the World's City Folks," Geographical Review, Vol. 21 (1931), 453.

[2] Walter Christaller, Die zentralen Orte in Süddeutschland (Jena: G. Fischer, 1933), translated by Carlisle W. Baskin as Central Places in Southern Germany (Englewood Cliffs, New Jersey: Prentice-Hall, 1966); Edward L. Ullman, "A Theory of Location for Cities," American Journal of Sociology, Vol. 46 (1941), 853-864.

urban centre—may be divided into two categories: those consumed within the area itself, and those consumed outside the area.[3] The terms nonbasic or city-serving refer to the production of goods consumed within the city itself, while the terms basic or city-forming refer to the production of goods which are exported beyond the city's boundaries.[4]

Although city-serving production is an important employer of the urban labour force, and accounts for the bulk of the economic activity in large cities, an urban centre's survival ultimately depends upon the performance of city-forming rather than city-serving activities. It is city-forming activities which bring income into a centre from the outside, thus providing its fundamental means of sustenance, and it is perhaps for this reason that geographers have given far more attention to city-forming than to city-serving production.[5]

Central place activities are a particular category of city-forming activities, and their distinctiveness is well brought out in a classification introduced some years ago by Harris and Ullman.[6] These writers divide city-forming activities into three broad classes, each class representing a different mechanism of urban support. First, towns are nodes on transportation networks, performing transshipment, break-of-bulk, maintenance, and other services in connection with the movement of people and goods across the face of the earth. Secondly, towns perform certain activities, other than transportation services, which are specialized in the sense that they do not directly affect the everyday behaviour of the individual consumer. In this category, two subclasses of functions may be recognized. First, there are activities which produce for a non-final market, and which thus face derived demands; examples are mining, manufacturing, and wholesaling. Secondly, there is the provi-

[3]Following standard usage, "good" throughout this study may refer either to a material item, or to a service, or to a combination of both.

[4]John W. Alexander, "The Basic-Nonbasic Concept of Urban Economic Functions," Economic Geography, Vol. 30 (1954), 246-261; Gunnar Alexandersson, The Industrial Structure of American Cities (Lincoln: University of Nebraska Press, 1956), pp. 14-20. Since "nonbasic" is faintly derogatory, Alexandersson's terms "city-serving" and "city-forming" are here preferred.

[5]Harold M. Mayer, "A Survey of Urban Geography," in The Study of Urbanization, edited by Philip M. Hauser and Leo F. Schnore (New York: Wiley, 1965), pp. 81-113.

[6]Chauncy D. Harris and Edward L. Ullman, "The Nature of Cities," Annals of the American Academy of Political and Social Science, Vol. 242 (1945), 7-17.

sion of resort amenities, which does cater directly to the consumer, but usually on a seasonal rather than a year-round basis. The final category of city-forming activities identified by Harris and Ullman is the supplying of goods directly to the population of a surrounding, contiguous area on a regular, year-round basis. It is this latter category of activities which is the concern of central place research.

Harris and Ullman suggest that each one of these three classes of city-forming activities, hypothetically operating in the absence of the other two classes, would produce its own distinctive spatial pattern of urban centres. Thus, the performance of transportation services, in itself, would give rise to linear arrangements of towns and cities. By contrast, the pattern created by the specialized activities in the second class would be one of considerable irregularity. The uneven distribution of such phenomena as ore deposits and ski slopes would ensure an irregular arrangement of towns performing mining and resort functions, and manufacturing centres also show a general tendency to cluster where natural and human resources are especially favourable.[7] Wholesale centres, it is true, might be expected to exhibit a more regular pattern, but wholesaling is a relatively minor employer compared to the other activities in its class. Finally, it is argued that direct consumer servicing, provided there is a rural population to serve, would tend to produce a uniform distribution of towns throughout the countryside.

In reality, the city-forming activities of a given town will usually fall into more than one of Harris and Ullman's three classes. It is thus unrealistic, in all but a very few cases, to refer to a particular town simply as a transportation centre, or a manufacturing centre, or a consumer service centre. These terms refer to aspects of urban support rather than to types of towns. One may, however, interpret the urban pattern of any sizeable area—say, Ontario—as being part linear in reflecting major transportation routes, part irregular where nature and economics have permitted the creation of mining, manufacturing, and resort towns, and part uniform where consumer service centres have developed in response to the demands of an agri-

---

[7]Gunnar Alexandersson, <u>Geography of Manufacturing</u> (Englewood Cliffs, New Jersey: Prentice-Hall, 1967).

cultural population. Given these distinctive elements in the pattern, it is a natural step for the geographer to attempt to separate the three sets of causative factors and examine them individually." Central place research thus achieves logical justification as that branch of urban network analysis concerned with the location, characteristics, and interrelationships of towns in their role as consumer service centres."

In addition to being overlapping elements in one and the same pattern, Harris and Ullman's three sets of city-forming factors act and react causally upon one another. For example, the alignment of major transportation routes may destroy the uniformity of the distribution of consumer service centres; and the latter type of centre, if large enough to provide an adequate labour force and other facilities, may attract manufacturing plants. These relationships, although obvious enough intuitively, cannot readily be translated into quantitative terms which would be of value in explaining any actual arrangement of towns. For this reason, the central place researcher prefers his "laboratory" to lie in an area where transport routes of more than local importance, and concentrations of specialized activities, are absent or at a minimum. In such an area, there is reasonable assurance that the urban pattern is due overwhelmingly to the consumer servicing aspect of urban support.

A central place, then, is simply a town viewed as a direct supplier of goods to consumers living outside the town's physical limits. It is understood that the town in question may have other city-forming functions besides central place activities, and that the internal, city-serving segment of the town's productive life is deliberately being disregarded.

The area containing the regular customers for a town's central place activities is commonly referred to as the town's umland.[8] Opinions differ as to how umlands are best delimited, but it is a matter of experience that the umlands of different centres vary both in size and in population, and it is equally evident that the variety of goods offered to consumers differs greatly among central places. In other words, places differ in the extent to which they function as consumer service centres.

[8]This term was first introduced by Allix over forty years ago; see André Allix, "The Geography of Fairs: Illustrated by Old-World Examples," Geographical Review, Vol. 12 (1922), 553.

The centrality of a town is a measure of the extent to which it is a central place. Centrality is usually expressed in terms of the variety of goods offered for sale.

In order to demonstrate the need for adequate measures of centrality, attention must be directed to the question of whether or not central places form a hierarchy. This is the most crucial problem in central place research, and it is vital that the meaning of "hierarchy" in this context be understood. In simple terms, a collection of entities comprises a hierarchy if it satisfies the following conditions. First, the entities may be arranged in tiers such that each member of every tier but the highest is subordinate to at least one member of some higher tier. Secondly, the responsibilities or capabilities of the members of a given tier must include the responsibilities or capabilities of the members of all lower tiers. Thirdly, the variation in responsibilities or capabilities among the members of a given tier must be less than the variations between that tier and its neighbouring tiers. And finally, the members of all tiers combined must form a complete system in the sense that all the entities which are ultimately subordinate to the members of the highest tier are included.

Military and ecclesiastical organizations in general are hierarchically structured systems. Consider the armed forces— for example, the navy. Commanders are subordinate to captains, and super-ordinate to lieutenant-commanders. The powers of a commander include those of all lower ranks. Commanders, qua commanders, are identical to one another and clearly distinct from both lieutenant-commanders and captains. And the navy itself is the complete system within which the hierarchical structure exists. Analogous conditions are fulfilled by church hierarchies.

A set of central places may also be examined in terms of the conditions necessary for a hierarchy to exist. Central place B may be said to be subordinate to central place A if the residents of B customarily rely on A for goods which B does not provide. Starting from an arbitrarily selected town, links of this type may be traced until the complete system of centres subordinate to the chosen central town has been identified. The central places in this system may then be examined to see whether they fall into tiers such that within-tier differences in the retail

7

and service complexity of the centres are smaller than between-tier differences.[9]

This last-mentioned condition involves an assessment of the relative commercial strengths of the centres in a central place system, and hence it is necessary for some acceptable method of measuring centrality to be devised. As noted earlier, the centrality of a central place is normally expressed in terms of the variety of goods supplied by the place. In practice, this involves taking an inventory of the retail and service establishments in the centre, and expressing the results either as the total number of such establishments, or as the number of distinct types of retail and service business, the latter being known as a count of functions. As an illustration, consider a hamlet containing a gas station and two general stores. Such a centre possesses three establishments, but only two functions.

Although the preparation of inventories of central place establishments is a fairly straightforward matter, there have been differences of opinion as to the form of inventory which best expresses differences in urban centrality. Both Smailes and Duncan have held the view that it is sufficient to consider only a short list of selected retail and service functions, basing the classification of towns on the presence, absence, and number of these functions in the centres studied.[10] Other workers, including King, Borchert and Adams, and Berry and his associates, have adopted an exhaustive approach, seeking to itemize every function present in the towns under investigation.[11] In addition to this difference between the selective and the exhaustive approach, some investigators, for example Smailes, have placed emphasis on differences in the numbers of business establishments in towns, while others, such as Berry, have worked

[9]This simplistic exposition of the concept of hierarchy in central place research is considerably expanded in the next chapter.

[10]Arthur E. Smailes, "The Urban Hierarchy in England and Wales," Geography, Vol. 29 (1944), 41-51; J. S. Duncan, "New Zealand Towns as Service Centres," New Zealand Geographer, Vol. 11 (1955), 119-138.

[11]Leslie J. King, "The Functional Role of Small Towns in Canterbury," Proceedings of the Third New Zealand Geography Conference (Palmerston North: New Zealand Geographical Society, 1961), pp. 139-149; John R. Borchert and Russell B. Adams, Trade Centers and Trade Areas of the Upper Midwest, Urban Report No. 3 (Minneapolis: Upper Midwest Research and Development Council, 1963); Brian J. L. Berry and William L. Garrison, "The Functional Bases of the Central Place Hierarchy," Economic Geography, Vol. 34 (1958), 145-154; Brian J. L. Berry, H. Gardiner Barnum, and Robert J. Tennant, "Retail Location and Consumer Behavior," Regional Science Association, Papers and Proceedings, Vol. 9 (1962), 65-106.

mainly with data on numbers of <u>functions</u>.

In regard to the distinction between selective and exhaustive inventories, there is no doubt that the latter, though more time-consuming to compile, provide the better expression of centrality differences. This is so because the exhaustive approach is bound to pick out finer distinctions between towns than is possible using a shortened list of functions. Since the answer to the question of the existence of a hierarchy of towns requires the development of the most accurate centrality measurements possible, it follows that the exhaustive approach is superior to the selective.

The question of whether to take inventory of functions or of establishments is not so easy to answer. In defence of using functions, it may be suggested that towns attract trade in proportion to the number of different goods they offer; while in defence of using establishments, it may be urged that trade is attracted in proportion to the amount of choice offered to the shopper with respect to individual goods. Intuitively, one feels that differences in numbers of functions (that is, in the variety of goods available), are more important among small centres, while differences in the amount of choice (that is, in numbers of establishments), are more significant among large towns. However, lacking any clear-cut empirical evidence on this matter, the safest course seems to be to consider data on both functions and establishments before coming to any conclusions, and this is the approach followed in the empirical portion of the present study.

With adequate measures of centrality available, it becomes possible to determine whether or not a central place system is hierarchically structured, and also to compare the spatial arrangements of centrality in different systems. Understanding of the sizes and spacing of towns over extensive areas is thus enhanced, and this is the ultimate goal of all central place research.

PLAN OF THE STUDY

The central theme of this study is formed of two related propositions. The first is that the question of the existence of a hierarchy of central places has not yet been fully answered, and the second is that further progress is dependent upon certain refinements in investigational technique. The argument in support of these propositions is most conveniently developed on the basis of a review of past research. Accordingly, chapter ii begins with an examination of classical central place theory, from which is then derived a set of diagnostic criteria for the identification of hierarchical structuring. Chapter iii investigates the extent to which these criteria have been employed in hierarchical classifications of towns proposed by previous investigators. In chapter iv, the same criteria are used as the basis for a discussion of the procedural refinements felt to be necessary for further progress in empirical studies. Chapters v and vi present a case study which illustrates the use of the proposed refinements, and chapter vi also serves to summarize and conclude the work.

II

Christaller's Theory and the Criteria of Hierarchical Structuring

Christaller's theoretical work on the size and spacing of central places first appeared in Germany in 1933.[1] In succeeding years, several résumés were published in English, and in 1957 a translation of the greater part of the original appeared as a doctoral dissertation.[2] Copies of this dissertation circulated widely among central place researchers, and in 1966 the translation was published in book form.[3] Christaller's work has therefore been quite readily accessible to English-speaking scholars for some years. Despite this fact, the original theory is reviewed here in detail in order to provide a sufficient background for the understanding of the diagnostic criteria of hierarchical structuring employed in this study.

[1]Walter Christaller, Die zentralen Orte in Süddeutschland (Jena: G. Fischer, 1933).

[2]Carlisle W. Baskin, "A Critique and Translation of Walter Christaller's Die zentralen Orte in Süddeutschland" (unpublished Ph.D. dissertation, University of Virginia, 1957). The résumés are: Edward L. Ullman, "A Theory of Location for Cities," American Journal of Sociology, Vol. 46 (1941), 853-864; Robert E. Dickinson, City Region and Regionalism (London: Routledge and Kegan Paul, 1947), chaps. ii and iii; Brian J. L. Berry and Allen Pred, Central Place Studies: A Bibliography of Theory and Applications (2nd edition; Philadelphia: Regional Science Research Institute, 1965), pp. 3-18; Arthur Getis and Judith Getis, "Christaller's Central Place Theory," Journal of Geography, Vol. 65 (1966), 220-226.

[3]Walter Christaller, Central Places in Southern Germany, translated by Carlisle W. Baskin (Englewood Cliffs, New Jersey: Prentice-Hall, 1966).

11

INITIAL FORMULATION
OF THE THEORY

Equilibrium of a Single Supplier

Christaller begins with the location economist's traditional medium, the isotropic plain. On this physiographically uniform surface, a farming population is assumed to be distributed at a constant density, and disposable income per farm family is assumed to be constant. In addition, movement is held to be equally unrestricted in all directions from all points, with transportation costs being directly proportional to distance travelled.

A further assumption is that the economy is essentially one of perfect competition. Individual transactions are relatively too small to affect the price of any commodity, and there is no collusion among suppliers. Centralized planning is absent, and "economic man" is the decision-making unit. However, in contrast to the non-spatial classical theory of perfect competition, Christaller's argument explicitly recognizes that location affects the competitive position of each supplier. Since each location is unique, each supplier is topologically a monopolist, rather than a perfect competitor. Indeed, the topological uniqueness of locations makes "spatial perfect competition" an impossibility. Christaller's theory should therefore be regarded as one in which the basic assumption of perfect competition is modified by explicit consideration of the factor of location. It is precisely this modification, incidentally, that makes central place research logically a branch of geography.[4]

Now let it be assumed that a particular good is made available for sale at one point on the isotropic plain. When a consumer buys this good, he must pay not only the purchase price, which is the same for all consumers, but also the cost of travelling from his farm to the supplier and back, which varies with his distance from the supplier. The actual cost of the good from the consumer's viewpoint therefore increases with distance from the point of supply.[5]

[4]The economist Chamberlin recognized that perfect competition was impossible given the uniqueness of locations, but the existence of locational monopolists was by no means the sole basis of his theory of monopolistic competition; see Edward H. Chamberlin, "The Product as an Economic Variable," Quarterly Journal of Economics, Vol. 67 (1953), 1-29.

[5]On this point, see also A. H. Anderson, "Space as a Social Cost," Journal of Farm Economics, Vol. 32 (1950), 411-430.

Following classical economic theory, the reasonable assumption is made that, as the cost of the good rises, so the quantity demanded declines. In spatial terms, this means that the quantity demanded declines as distance from the supplier increases. Sooner or later, a point will be reached where the demand for the good is zero, since farmers are not willing to pay the transportation costs necessary to reach the supplier. In this simple case, the supplier's market area will have a circular perimeter, beyond which the demand for his good is zero. The radius of this market area is termed the range of the good.

It will not be possible for the supplier to stay in business unless he is patronized by a certain minimum number of consumers. If the number of patrons drops below this critical level, the supplier will not be able to meet his own costs (including what the economist terms "normal profits"), and his enterprise will fail. This minimum number of consumers necessary to support the supply of a particular good is termed the good's threshold.

It follows that the threshold of a good sets a minimum value upon the range of that good. Consider a hypothetical good which consumers are not willing to travel very far to obtain. It is conceivable that a supplier of this good would discover that the number of consumers living within the range of the good was smaller than the threshold number of consumers needed to support his firm. Assuming for the moment that the supplier is a monopolist, he might contrive to increase the range of the good, and hence the size of his clientele, by lowering his price; but it is still possible for the shut-down price to be reached before the range is large enough to encompass the threshold number of consumers. Under these conditions, the supplier would go out of business. Stating the matter in general terms, the supply of a good is economically feasible only when the maximum distance that consumers are willing to travel to buy the good is equal to, or greater than, the radius of a circle containing the threshold population appropriate to that good.[6]

[6]Particular attention is given to the concepts of range and threshold in the following papers: Brian J. L. Berry and William L. Garrison, "A Note on Central Place Theory and the Range of a Good," Economic Geography, Vol. 34 (1958), 304-311; Robert C. Mayfield, "The Range of a Central Good in the Indian Punjab," Annals of the Association of American Geographers, Vol. 53 (1963), 38-49.

The range of a good is thus seen to have an upper and a lower limit. The upper limit is determined by the maximum distance consumers will travel to obtain the good, and the lower limit is determined by the good's threshold. However, the ac-tual limit of the range will be determined by spatial competition among several suppliers of the same good. This raises the question of the arrangement of suppliers and market areas on the plain when more than one supplier is present.

Equilibrium of Many Suppliers
Let it be assumed that as many suppliers as possible locate on the plain. This means that each supplier must be as close to his competitors as the space-economy will permit. Since each supplier has a circular market area, the problem may be visu-alized as that of packing circular plates on a table so that their centres are as close to one another as possible. Inspection shows that the appropriate arrangement is for each plate to be tangent to six surrounding plates, their centres being located on a triangular lattice, as shown in Figure 1. Moreover, since it is specified that as many suppliers locate on the plain as pos-sible, the size of each market area will be minimized. In other words, the range of the good will be at its lower limit, set by the threshold required to make the suppliers economically vi-able.

Consumers located in the quasi-triangular interstices be-tween the tangent circles in Figure 1 may patronize any one of three adjacent suppliers with approximately equal ease. For the moment, the patronage of these consumers may be regarded

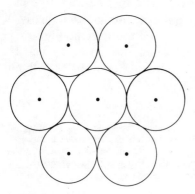

Figure 1. Ideal Arrangement of Suppliers with Circular Mar-ket Areas

14

as accruing to the suppliers as "excess profits"; that is, profits over and above the normal profits of economic theory. The interstices between the circles will later be removed by replacing the circles with hexagons, so that every part of the plain is assigned to one particular supplier. The shape of the market areas, however, is less important than the pattern of the locations of the supply points, and the temporary retention of circular market areas makes it easier to present the next steps in the argument.

With suppliers packed as closely as possible, then, the ideal arrangement is for each supplier to be equidistant from six of his competitors. It is of historical interest that this triangular arrangement of competing suppliers was intuitively recognized as theoretically sound by the American rural sociologist Galpin almost two decades before the initial appearance of Christaller's work. Galpin's contribution was isolated, however, and did not immediately become part of the general corpus of location theory, and thus it is Christaller who is rightly regarded as the fountainhead of central place research.[7]

Development of a Hierarchical Pattern

Up to this point, the Christallerian landscape has been developed as one in which all the farmers on the plain are within the range of one particular good, a good which is being supplied by the maximum possible number of economically viable suppliers. Consider now a long list of goods of various kinds, each of which is to be supplied by a distinct set of establishments. No doubt each set of suppliers could locate separately in the manner already described, but it is more rational to assume that each set will pay attention to the behaviour of the other sets. In particular, each set of suppliers may be assumed to wish to occupy, so far as possible, locations possessing some comparative advantage. This assumption implies that the total number of supply points—that is, agglomerations of suppliers of different goods—will be kept to a minimum.

Different goods have different threshold values. Bread, for example, has a lower threshold than television sets, and

[7]Charles J. Galpin, The Social Anatomy of an Agricultural Community, Research Bulletin No. 34 (Madison: University of Wisconsin Agricultural Experiment Station, 1915).

television sets have a lower threshold than the services of a psychiatrist. Goods may thus be ranked according to their thresholds. Suppose the isotropic plain is to be supplied with n different goods, and let these be ranked from 1 to n in ascending order of threshold requirements. Let supply points for good n be called A centres, and let these centres locate on the plain in accordance with the assumptions made earlier. The A centres will thus form a triangular lattice of points on the plain, and their number will be governed by the number of minimum-sized threshold market areas which can be carved out of the plain for suppliers of good n.[8]

Consider now good $(n - 1)$, the good having the second highest threshold requirement. The suppliers of this good will maximize their accessibility to their customers if they locate in the A centres, which have already been established. In this way, no new supply points are added to the plain, and the aggregate mileage travelled by consumers to obtain either or both goods is not increased.

Since good $(n - 1)$ has a lower threshold than good n, spatial competition will determine its range from each centre, and the suppliers of good $(n - 1)$ will be in a position to earn, in the aggregate, greater excess profits than the suppliers of good n.

The same reasoning applies to succeeding goods with progressively lower thresholds. The suppliers will continue to locate in the A centres, and as threshold requirements decrease so the aggregate volume of excess profits earned will rise. The excess profits, for the suppliers of a given good, represent simply the purchasing power of consumers living between the A centres, but outside imaginary circles centred on the A centres with radii defined by the threshold of the good in question. Figure 2 makes this relationship clear.

As goods with successively lower thresholds are added, a good is bound to be reached—say, good $(n - p)$—for which the interstitial buying power available as excess profits will in fact be large enough to permit suppliers of good $(n - p)$ to establish themselves not only in the A centres, but also in the interstices between these centres. In other words, the purchasing power

---

[8]In order to facilitate later comparison, the notation used in this discussion is similar to that used in Brian J. L. Berry and William L. Garrison, "Recent Developments of Central Place Theory," Regional Science Association, Papers and Proceedings, Vol. 4 (1958), 107-120.

16

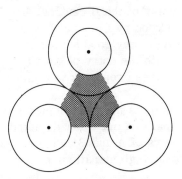

Figure 2. The Location of Excess Profits

Large circles are threshold market areas for suppliers of the good with the highest threshold. Small circles are threshold market areas for suppliers of good G, a good with a lower threshold. The shaded area provides excess profits to suppliers of good G.

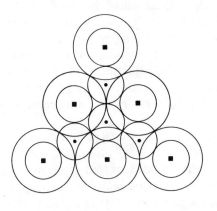

Figure 3. The Viability of Interstitial Locations

■ A—centre   • B—centre

Large circles are threshold market areas for suppliers of the good with the highest threshold. Small circles are threshold market areas for suppliers of the hierarchical marginal good of the B order.

located in the interstices between suppliers of good $(n - p)$ in the $\underline{A}$ centres will be equal to the threshold requirement of good $(n - p)$. A second set of centres, which may be called $\underline{B}$ centres, will thus appear. Each $\underline{B}$ centre will be located at the centre of the triangle formed by three adjacent $\underline{A}$ centres, as shown in Figure 3.

Good ($\underline{n}$ - $\underline{p}$), which marks the entry of the $\underline{B}$ centres, has been termed a hierarchical marginal good by Berry and Garrison.[9] The $\underline{B}$ centres cannot supply any good having a higher threshold than good ($\underline{n}$ - $\underline{p}$). With the entry of good ($\underline{n}$ - $\underline{p}$), also, excess profits accruing to suppliers drop back to a minimum (compare Figures 2 and 3).

Though the Christallerian landscape is not yet complete, two significant features of the emerging pattern must now be noted. The first concerns the relative numbers of $\underline{A}$ and $\underline{B}$ centres, and the second their relative complexity as agglomerations of suppliers.

Each $\underline{A}$ centre on the plain is surrounded by six other $\underline{A}$ centres. Alternatively, each $\underline{A}$ centre is the apex of six equilateral triangles having other $\underline{A}$ centres at their other apexes. Thus, each $\underline{A}$ centre is also surrounded by six $\underline{B}$ centres, one located at the centre of each of the equilateral triangles just described. However, each of these six $\underline{B}$ centres is equidistant from three $\underline{A}$ centres. Hence, for every $\underline{A}$ centre, the plain as a whole contains (6 x 1/3) or two $\underline{B}$ centres. This ratio, as will be shown, is significant for the derivation of the criteria of hierarchical structuring used in this study.

Secondly, it must be noted that each $\underline{A}$ centre can supply all goods from good $\underline{n}$ to good ($\underline{n}$ - $\underline{p}$) and below, while no $\underline{B}$ centre can supply any good having a higher threshold than good ($\underline{n}$ - $\underline{p}$). In other words, there is a clear distinction between $\underline{A}$ and $\underline{B}$ centres in regard to their degree of complexity as service centres. In fact, all $\underline{A}$ centres are alike, and all $\underline{B}$ centres are alike, and the difference in complexity between the $\underline{A}$ and $\underline{B}$ groups is necessarily greater than the difference within either group. This feature is also important for the derivation of criteria of hierarchical structuring.

Without affecting the logic of the argument, Figure 3 may be redrawn in a less cluttered form by eliminating the quasi-triangular interstices between the sets of tangent circles. This may be achieved simply by replacing each circle with its circumscribed hexagon, as shown in Figure 4. Christaller, who did use hexagons rather than circles in some of his illustrations, seems to have arrived at the hexagonal shape by just this pro-

[9]Berry and Garrison, "Recent Developments of Central Place Theory," 112.

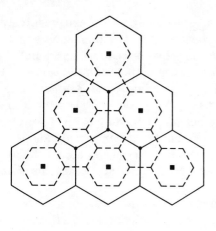

Figure 4. The Arrangement of A and B Centres with Hexagonal Market Areas

■ A—centre   • B—centre

The market areas in this figure are the circumscribed hexagons of the circular market areas in Figure 3.

cess of tidying up the diagram.[10] However, the use of the hexagon may be justified by arbitrarily postulating that no areas on the plain are either unserved or served by more than one supplier. Market areas must therefore be either hexagons, squares, or equilateral triangles, since these are the only space-filling polygons having radial symmetry; and of these three shapes, the hexagon departs least from the circular ideal. It should be noted, moreover, that the introduction of the hexagon implies that excess profits can no longer be earned by the suppliers of the hierarchical marginal goods n and $(n - p)$, since interstitial areas no longer exist between the threshold market areas for suppliers of these goods.[11]

The same logic which has been used to account for the appearance on the plain of B centres may now be used to justify the appearance of lower orders of C centres, D centres, and so

[10]Christaller, Central Places in Southern Germany; compare especially the figures on pp. 61 and 66.
[11]Strictly speaking, the introduction of the hexagon involves a slight reduction in the distances between supply centres, since these distances are determined by the sizes of market areas, and a circle is slightly smaller than the hexagon which circumscribes it.

19

forth. Continuing from good $(n - p)$ to goods with progressively lower thresholds, the $\underline{A}$ and $\underline{B}$ centres will be adopted as supply points until a certain good—say $(n - q)$—is reached for which the interstitial purchasing power, located between the threshold market areas for suppliers of $(n - q)$ in the $\underline{A}$ and $\underline{B}$ centres, is equal to the threshold for good $(n - q)$. Good $(n - q)$ is the hierarchical marginal good for the set of $\underline{C}$ centres, each of which supplies good $(n - q)$ and all goods having lower thresholds. Further down the list of goods, good $(n - r)$ is the hierarchical marginal good for the set of $\underline{D}$ centres, good $(n - s)$ for the set of $\underline{E}$ centres, and so forth.

Each time a new set of centres is added to the plain, the members of that set will be located at the centres of all triangles formed by adjacent pre-existing supply points. Thus each $\underline{D}$ centre, for example, is located at the centre of a triangle which has an $\underline{A}$, $\underline{B}$, or $\underline{C}$ centre at each of its apexes. When all centres are considered simultaneously, without regard to rank, it follows that the overall pattern is always that of a triangular lattice. The arrangement of several ranks relative to one another is easier to visualize graphically than to describe in words, and is shown in Figure 5. Note how each centre is symmetrically surrounded by six centres of the next lower order, and how the market areas of lower order centres nest within those of successively higher order centres.[12]

Characteristics of the Hierarchy

It was shown above that the plain as a whole contains two $\underline{B}$ centres for every $\underline{A}$ centre. Since the method by which successive orders of centres are added does not change, it will always be true that the number of centres in a given order will equal twice the number of centres in all higher orders combined. The ratios of numbers of centres in successive orders, in other words, run as follows:

$$\underline{A} : \underline{B} : \underline{C} : \underline{D} : \underline{E} : \underline{F} = 1 : 2 : 6 : 18 : 54 : 162$$

These ratios may be verified by an examination of the market area of the highest order centre shown in Figure 5; assume

---

[12]The terms "city," "town," "village," and "hamlet" appearing in Figure 5 and later illustrations serve merely as convenient labels for the levels of the hierarchical structure, and are without implication regarding the legal status of the centres.

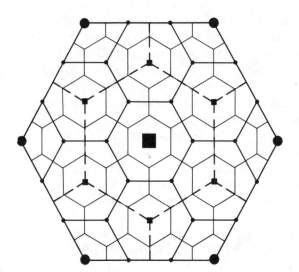

■	————	City and city level umland
●	— — —	Town and town level umland
▪	————	Village and village level umland
•	————	Hamlet and hamlet level umland

Figure 5. Christaller's <u>Versorgungsprinzip</u> Model

that this centre of "city" status is an <u>A</u> centre. At the corners
of this <u>A</u> centre's market area lie six <u>B</u> centres. Each <u>B</u> centre, however, is located at the junction of the market areas of
three <u>A</u> centres (only one <u>A</u> centre appears in Figure 5), so that
each <u>B</u> centre may be counted as only 1/3 in calculating the numerical ratio of <u>A</u> to <u>B</u> centres. The <u>A</u> centre thus has (6 x 1/3)
or the equivalent of two <u>B</u> centres within its market area. The
expression (6 x 1/3) may be taken to mean that the probability
of residents of a <u>B</u> centre shopping in a particular <u>A</u> centre is
1/3, since three <u>A</u> centres of equal attractiveness are available
to them.

Focussing now on lower orders, it is clear that six <u>C</u> centres lie wholly within the <u>A</u> centre's market area. The <u>D</u> centres, however, pose a problem analogous to that of the <u>B</u> centres.

Twelve D centres are wholly within the A centre's market area, but an additional twelve lie exactly on the boundary. Each of these latter twelve is equidistant from two A centres, and each must therefore be counted as 1/2 in calculating the ratio of A to D centres. The A centre thus has $(12 + (12 \times 1/2))$ or the equivalent of 18 D centres within its market area. Putting all these figures together, the ratios given above are obtained:

$$A : B : C : D = 1 : 2 : 6 : 18$$

The series could be extended by graphical extension of Figure 5.

It must now be noted that each A centre on the plain, since it supplies all goods, functions not only at the A level but also at all lower levels. Similarly, each B centre functions at all levels except the A level; each C centre functions at all levels except B and A; and so forth. Thus, the ratios presented above express only the numbers of centres functioning at the stated level and at no higher level. If each centre is counted not only at its highest level, but also at all lower levels, the number series is cumulative and runs as follows:

$$A : B : C : D : E : F = 1 : 3 : 9 : 27 : 81 : 243$$

These figures may be interpreted as follows. The market area of one A centre contains, among others, nine centres functioning at the C level. In fact, one of these nine is the A centre itself, and two others are made up of the one-third portions of the six peripheral B centres. The remaining six are centres which do not function at any level higher than the C level.

Christaller identified the pattern described above as the Versorgungsprinzip or "marketing principle" landscape. This landscape is properly regarded as a spatial economic model. Like all models, it is an idealized representation of certain aspects of reality, and it may be used as a source of concepts and principles which can give direction to empirical work. In this respect, the significance of the Versorgungsprinzip model is the fact that its essential features may be employed as diagnostic criteria for the identification of hierarchical structuring among real central places.

DIAGNOSTIC CRITERIA OF
HIERARCHICAL STRUCTURING

The fundamental characteristics of the ideal central place hierarchy depicted in Figure 5 are seven in number, and they may
briefly be identified as follows:
      (1) spatial interdependence of centres
      (2) functional wholeness of the system
      (3) discrete stratification of centrality
      (4) interstitial placement of orders
      (5) incremental baskets of goods
      (6) a minimum of three orders
      (7) a numerical pyramid in order membership
Two general points must be made. First, in using these characteristics as diagnostic criteria of a hierarchy, extreme rigidity of interpretation could well hinder rather than assist
empirical research. Hence, the criteria are designed to incorporate the general rather than the specific features of the model.
Secondly, the present section shows how these criteria are derived from central place theory, but does not investigate how
they may best be made operational for empirical studies. The
latter problem is discussed fully in chapter iv.

    Consider once more the A centre and its market area shown
in Figure 5. Since all goods are provided to all consumers with
a minimum of consumer travel, each B, C, and D centre within
the A centre's market area depends upon at least one other centre within that same area for goods which it does not itself provide. Movements of shoppers and of delivery vans among the
various centres literally connect the centres together and create
a system of towns. For the A centre itself, these connections
exist directly or indirectly with every centre lying within its
market area. In other words, the network is characterized by
spatial interdependence of centres. The places are all members
of the A centre's central place system, which gains its identity
through the fact that the member centres all rely on the A centre
for the supply of certain goods.

    The rationale for this notion of system in central place an-
alysis lies in the fact that the commercial development of any
particular central place is limited by the level of functional
complexity attained in the centre or centres to which it is tributary. Since some suppliers require larger numbers of con-

sumers for their support than others, it is impossible for certain of the goods provided by a large town to be provided by small centres in that town's umland. Thus, the functional complexity of a town at a given point in time acts as a brake on the functional development of lesser centres which rely on it. The group of places tributary to a selected central town forms a system of centres in which the larger members draw trade from the smaller, and at the same time restrict their commercial growth. This interdependence gives the spatial system its identity.

A given centre's system is not indefinite in extent. Returning to Figure 5, all places lying inside the $\underline{A}$ centre's market area are members of its system, but places lying beyond the market area boundary have no links with the $\underline{A}$ centre and are therefore parts of other systems. Centres lying exactly on the boundary are members of either two or three comparable $\underline{A}$-level systems, but these systems have no connection with one another except through the existence of the borderline centres. In the real world, truly borderline centres are comparatively rare, and when found can be regarded as special cases. Generally speaking, therefore, a central place system is composed of all the centres lying within the market area of a selected central place. It is this complete functional system which should be the unit of analysis in the search for real hierarchies. Wholeness of the system is the second criterion of hierarchical structuring here employed.

It is acknowledged that this systems concept is not explicit in Christaller's original work. However, it is certainly present in principle, and must necessarily be invoked to provide a satisfactory solution to the problem of identifying a study area for empirical research. It is worth noting, in this connection, that the areal extent of a complete central place system is in general unlikely to coincide with the territory occupied by one or more political subdivisions.

Consider now the relative functional complexity of the various orders of centres in the model. The $\underline{A}$ centre supplies all goods from good $\underline{n}$, the good with the highest threshold, to good 1, the good with the lowest threshold. The $\underline{B}$ centres are unable to supply any good with a higher threshold than good $(\underline{n} - \underline{p})$, and there are thus several goods which are supplied only from the $\underline{A}$ centre and not from centres of any other level. These goods

24

set the $\underline{A}$ centre clearly apart from the $\underline{B}$ centres and centres of all lower levels. Similarly, the $\underline{C}$ centres are unable to supply any good with a higher threshold than good $(n - q)$, so there are several goods—with thresholds lying between those of goods $(n - p)$ and $(n - q)$—which are supplied only from the $\underline{B}$ centres (including the $\underline{A}$ centre in its capacity as a $\underline{B}$ centre), and not from $\underline{C}$ centres or centres of any lower level. This argument may be extended to cover all levels of centres included in the model. Therefore, since the centres at any one level are functionally identical to one another, it follows that the differences in functional complexity between the various levels are greater than the differences within each level; the latter, in fact, are zero. A third criterion for hierarchical structuring is thus derived; namely, that the central places in the system under investigation must exhibit discrete stratification of centrality.

The importance of this third criterion cannot be too strongly emphasized. The notion of clear-cut groups of centres is intrinsic to the concept of hierarchical structuring, yet it has been one of the chief roots of disagreements in the literature. In particular, the idea of definite orders of central places has been opposed by the concept of a smooth continuum of urban importance, and the debate on this issue is analyzed fully later. At present it is only necessary that the distinction between a hierarchy and a continuum be clearly understood.

It is a matter of observation that, as the size of towns increases, so does their complexity as retail and service centres.[13] However, it is not immediately obvious whether the increases in size and functional complexity from town to town are smooth and gradual, or whether, as the concept of hierarchy implies, there are "plateaus" on which towns tend to cluster. It is sometimes implied that the term "hierarchy" signifies merely the existence of fewer large centres than small ones.[14] Such a view is subject to such rapid empirical testing that to accept it would virtually eliminate central place research as a field with a geographic problem to investigate. This view,

[13]C. Schettler, "Relation of City-Size to Economic Services," American Sociological Review, Vol. 8 (1943), 60-62; Colin Clark, "The Economic Functions of a City in Relation to Its Size," Econometrica, Vol. 13 (1945), 97-113.

[14]See, for example, P. S. Florence, "Economic Efficiency in the Metropolis," in The Metropolis in Modern Life, edited by Robert M. Fisher (New York: Doubleday, 1955), pp. 115-118; also Otis D. Duncan and others, Metropolis and Region (Baltimore: Johns Hopkins Press, 1960), pp. 56-69.

however, is not acceptable. As Murphy has recently noted, "the idea of distinct classes with real breaks between them is rooted in Christaller's work and is in fact inherent in his theory."[15]

Turning again to Figure 5, it is clear from the manner in which Christaller's model is constructed that the centres operating at any given level of complexity form a regular geometric pattern on the landscape. Moreover, the centres at successively lower levels are regularly located in the interstices of this geometric pattern. Notice, on Figure 5, that the step-by-step removal of successively higher orders (beginning with the removal of the hamlets), would result in a progressive change in the scale of the pattern, with no change in the form of the pattern. This distinctive feature is adopted as the fourth criterion for the identification of a hierarchy; namely, the criterion of interstitial placement of orders. It may be noted at this point that, of all the seven diagnostic criteria used in this study, the criterion of interstitial placement of orders is the most difficult to define operationally for the purposes of empirical work.

The criterion of interstitial placement of orders is intimately related to that of discrete stratification of centrality. The closeness of the relationship may be illustrated by consideration of a layout of centres identical to that shown in Figure 5 with one exception; namely, that one of the villages (C centre), has the stature of a town (B centre), in terms of its functional complexity. Should this centre be classed as a town by virtue of its functional compexity, or as a village by virtue of its location? Clearly, it belongs on the "town plateau" as regards the stratification of centrality, but equally clearly it occupies an interstitial location in which one expects to find a centre of only village stature.

How the offending centre is labelled does not affect the question, "Why is this centre of town stature in this village location?" The classificatory dilemma, however, emphasizes the fact that the concept of a central place hierarchy has an inescapable spatial component. The relative functional complexity of places

---

[15]Raymond E. Murphy, The American City: An Urban Geography (New York: McGraw-Hill, 1966), p. 96.

simply cannot be dissociated from their relative locations.

The remaining three criteria of an ideal urban hierarchy are those of incremental baskets of goods, a minimum of three orders, and a numerical pyramid in order membership. These criteria are less complex than the preceding four.

The criterion of incremental baskets of goods is derived from the fact that a functionally complex centre in the Christaller model is distinguished from a simpler centre not by providing an entirely different array of goods, but by providing the same goods as the simpler centre plus an incremental basket of different goods in addition. In other words, the list of goods supplied by a given centre includes all goods supplied by lower order centres in the same system. In practice, the use of this particular characteristic as a criterion for the identification of an urban hierarchy creates far fewer problems than the use of the other characteristics discussed above. The principle of incremental baskets of goods, though perhaps never found to perfection, is invariably closely approximated in reality.

Perhaps less definitely essential as a criterion of hierarchical structuring is the existence of a minimum of three orders of centres. By focussing attention on an appropriately small village, one could isolate a central place system containing only two orders: the central village and a handful of hamlets which it dominates. For aesthetic reasons, one hesitates to dignify such a simple structure with the name of hierarchy. This type of system is likely to be very common in reality, but it exists at a scale too elemental to allow any broad generalizations on the structure of urban systems to be formulated. On the other hand, such a two-tiered system could certainly satisfy all the other conditions for a hierarchy, and it may be quibbling to rule it beyond the pale. Perhaps the compromise of terming such a structure a "one-step hierarchy" is acceptable.

Though partly a matter of aesthetics, this requirement that at least three orders be present may also be derived from Christaller's model. The only limit to the number of orders which may appear in the model is the size of the threshold of good 1 (the good having the lowest threshold), relative to the size of the threshold of good n (the good having the highest threshold). Once good 1 is being supplied, there is obviously no call for further sets of interstitial centres to be added to the landscape. Since the threshold of good n is likely to be many times larger than the threshold of good 1, there is every reason to believe that at least three orders of centres are necessary to ensure the supply of all goods. Christaller's original diagram of the ideal landscape depicted five orders, and in the text he indicated that, on the basis of the actual ranges of goods in Bavaria, at least seven orders of central places could be expected to occur.[16]

Finally, there is the criterion of <u>a numerical pyramid in order membership</u>. To say that such a pyramid exists is to say that each order of centres contains more places than the next higher order. In the preceding section, it was shown that the ratios of numbers of places in successive orders within the market area of an <u>A</u> centre in the <u>Versorgungsprinzip</u> model are as follows:

$$\underline{A} : \underline{B} : \underline{C} : \underline{D} : \underline{E} : \underline{F} = 1 : 2 : 6 : 18 : 54 : 162$$

Since the <u>A</u> centre's market area defines the system which is the unit of study, the general statement can be made that, in an ideal hierarchy, the numbers of centres at successive levels do form a pyramidal series. It is suggested, however, that insistence upon a fixed formula expressing the numbers of centres in successive ranks would represent too rigid a position for empirical investigations. The real world rarely approaches the conditions of the isotropic plain assumed in the model, and real urban systems usually contain some functions other than central place activities. This final criterion is therefore designed, like all the others, to incorporate the general rather than the specific features of the model.

The seven fundamental criteria for the identification of a hierarchical system of central places are thus derived directly from the basic model formulated by the father of central place theory. The remaining sections of this chapter will examine additional aspects of the theory. While the <u>Versorgungsprinzip</u> model is not the only possible theoretical landscape, it will become evident that the basic concept of a hierarchy, and the criteria described above for its identification, appear to stand unchallenged.

---

[16]Christaller, <u>Central Places in Southern Germany</u>, pp. 58-68, especially the figure on p. 66 and the table on p. 67.

An important feature of the isotropic plain with which Christaller began his discussion was that movement was equally unrestricted in all directions from all points. Using this assumption, no attention had to be given at any stage to the question of the alignment of transport routes. It must have proved difficult, however, for Christaller to banish this question from his thoughts, for in addition to the model described above he presented a model based on a Verkehrsprinzip or "traffic principle."

The logic of this second model was not given in detail by Christaller, but must have been identical to that of the Versorgungsprinzip model up to the point at which the A centres were located evenly spaced across the plain. It was then postulated that these A centres would be connected by major transport routes, which in turn would influence the positioning of subsequent supply centres. It was felt that the most rational location for the second set of centres—the B centres—was no longer at the centres of the triangles formed by the A places, as in the previous model, but at the midpoints of the routes connecting the A places to one another. This relationship is illustrated in Figure 6. Given that transport routes link the higher level centres, this midpoint location has also been recognized as viable for lower order places by Godlund.[17]

With the B centres thus located, new roads were presumed to be built linking them with one another, so that once again every pair of adjacent centres on the plain was linked by a transport route. The third set of centres—the C centres—was then located at the midpoints of the routes between every pair of preexisting centres. Each C centre thus lay either midway between two B centres or midway between a B centre and an A centre. More roads were built, and more sets of centres added, until a multiple-tiered system of centres had appeared as shown in Figure 7.

Although the arrangement of centres and market areas in this Verkehrsprinzip model differs from that of the Versorgungsprinzip model, inspection shows that the system is still char-

---

[17]Sven Godlund, "Bus Services, Hinterlands, and the Location of Urban Settlements in Sweden, Specially in Scania," Lund Studies in Geography, Series B, No. 3 (1951), 14-24.

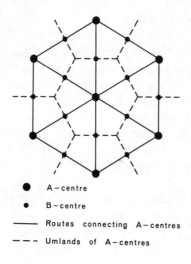

Figure 6. Location of B Centres
on Routes Connecting A Centres

● A-centre

• B-centre

—— Routes connecting A-centres

--- Umlands of A-centres

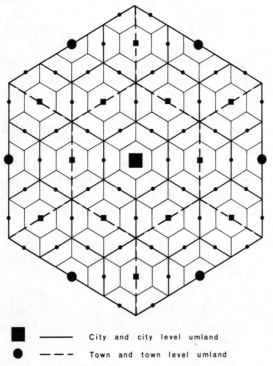

■ —— City and city level umland

● --- Town and town level umland

▪ —— Village and village level umland

• —— Hamlet and hamlet level umland

Figure 7. Christaller's <u>Verkehrsprinzip</u> Model

acterized by the seven features derived from the Versorgungs-prinzip model for use as criteria of hierarchical structuring.
In particular, discrete stratification of functional complexity is ensured by the discontinuous reduction in the numbers of consumers serviced by the members of successively lower orders, as represented by the different sizes of market areas in Figure 7. The only significant difference between the two models, apart from the changed spatial arrangement of the centres, lies in the ratios of the numbers of places in successive orders. An analysis of Figure 7 similar to that carried out earlier for Figure 5 shows that the ratios run as follows:

$$\underline{A} : \underline{B} : \underline{C} : \underline{D} : \underline{E} = 1 : 3 : 12 : 48 : 192$$

Or alternatively, if each centre is counted not only at its highest level, but also at all lower levels, the sequence is as follows:

$$\underline{A} : \underline{B} : \underline{C} : \underline{D} : \underline{E} = 1 : 4 : 16 : 64 : 256$$

It is clear that the model still exhibits a pyramidal sequence of numbers of central places in successive ranks.

In addition to the marketing and traffic principles of central place organization, Christaller considered the operation of a third principle, termed the Absonderungsprinzip or "separation principle." Both of the models described above contain certain centres which are located exactly on the boundaries between competing centres of higher rank. Christaller suggested that the divided economic allegiance of such borderline centres did not accord well with the ideals of effective political administration and control, and he introduced some empirical evidence to indicate that local and regional seats of government in general hold sway over whole numbers of lesser centres, with the boundaries of administrative areas lying between centres rather than through them. However, despite a gallant attempt, Christaller found himself unable to draw a model based on this principle without considerable distortion of the regular arrangement of centres and market areas which is so notable a feature of the previous models.[18] In fact, a model based on the Absonderungsprinzip can indeed be drawn, with the central places on the usual triangular lattice, with perfectly hexagonal market areas, and with no centre lying on any market area boundary. This model appears as Figure 8.

[18]Christaller, Central Places in Southern Germany, diagrams on pp. 78 and 79.

31

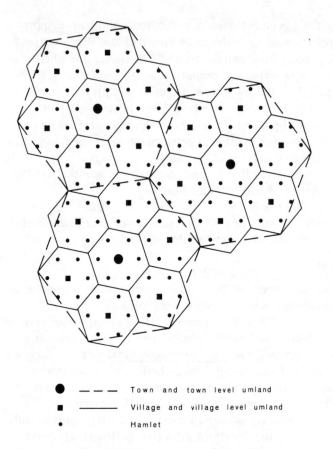

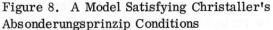

● — — — Town and town level umland

■ ————— Village and village level umland

● Hamlet

Figure 8. A Model Satisfying Christaller's
Absonderungsprinzip Conditions

In this Absonderungsprinzip model, the positions of lower-
order centres in the interstices between higher-order centres
cannot be rationalized as rigorously as in the previous models.
However, if the retention of a perfectly triangular lattice of
centres is taken as a fixed requirement, regardless of the number of orders present, it may be observed that the size and or-
ientation of every market area is determined by the condition
that no centre lies on any market area boundary. This gives
rise to a system in which the numbers of centres in successive
orders run as follows:

$$\underline{A} : \underline{B} : \underline{C} : \underline{D} : \underline{E} = 1 : 6 : 42 : 294 : 2,058$$

Or alternatively, if each centre is counted not only at its highest level, but also at all lower levels, the sequence becomes:

$$\underline{A} : \underline{B} : \underline{C} : \underline{D} : \underline{E} = 1 : 7 : 49 : 343 : 2,401$$

The system is otherwise similar to the Versorgungsprinzip and Verkehrsprinzip systems, and exhibits the full range of features adopted in this study as diagnostic criteria of hierarchical structuring.

A RESTATEMENT OF
CHRISTALLERIAN THEORY

In an important paper published in 1958, Berry and Garrison demonstrate that

> . . . whatever the distribution of purchasing power (and whether in open countryside or within a large metropolis) a hierarchical spatial structure of central places supplying central goods will emerge.[19]

This statement removes the fundamental Christallerian assumption that disposable income is distributed on the isotropic plain with constant density. In other words, the plain need not be isotropic in order for a hierarchy to appear. The manner in which Berry and Garrison arrive at this conclusion merits close attention.

Berry and Garrison's reasoning closely parallels the basic Christallerian argument already presented. A significant difference, however, lies in the fact that no regular geometrical pattern is ascribed to the locations of the first centres to appear in the model. With good $\underline{n}$ as the good having the highest threshold, Berry and Garrison describe the initial set of locations as follows:

> As many $\underline{A}$ centres will exist in the area as there are threshold sales levels to support firms supplying good $\underline{n}$. These firms compete spatially, hence are distributed so as to supply their own threshold most efficiently.[20]

This may be taken to mean that the $\underline{A}$ centres, while not necessarily equidistant from one another, are nevertheless located so that each is equally accessible to an identical amount of consumer purchasing power. Retaining the Christallerian

[19]Berry and Garrison, "Recent Developments of Central Place Theory," 111; italics in original.
[20]Ibid., 111-112.

assumption that disposable income per farm family is constant, this implies that the A centres will be close together where the farm population is dense, and farther apart where it is sparse. An approximate impression of the resulting arrangement of A centres may be obtained by imagining that the original isotropic plain is represented by a rubber sheet, and that the A centres are printed on this sheet in their original pattern of locations at the apexes of equilateral triangles. Now imagine that the sheet is stretched by various amounts in various directions. This has the effect of varying the density of disposable income, and with it the spacing of the A centres. However, it remains true that each centre draws its support from an identical threshold amount of consumer purchasing power.

With the landscape developed in this manner, the A centres will lie at varying distances from one another, but they will still be located so that each centre is surrounded by approximately six others. This follows from Berry and Garrison's implication that the A centres, which are as numerous as is economically feasible, will locate as close to one another as possible. The packing problem is analogous to that described earlier for plates on a table, but now the plates are of different sizes, depending upon the density of purchasing power in various parts of the area. An example of the type of landscape which results is shown in Figure 9.

Of great importance to the continuation of the argument is the further implication that all triangles formed by joining three neighbouring A centres will contain approximately equal amounts of purchasing power, even though these triangles, as shown in Figure 9, differ from one another in area. For it is in these triangles that the second set of centres—the B centres—will appear, and if the threshold purchasing power available to these B centres is not constant throughout the area, then there is no reason to suppose that all B centres will be of equal functional complexity.

Once the A centres are established, Berry and Garrison's reasoning follows that of Christaller. Goods with lower thresholds than good n are supplied from the A centres by firms which can earn excess profits from the patronage of consumers living in the interstitial areas between the A centres. But sooner or later a good is reached—say, good $(n - i)$—for which the amounts of interstitial purchasing power, located between threshold mar-

34

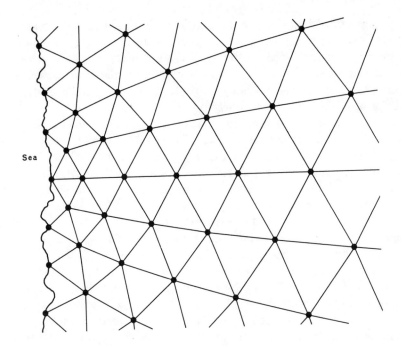

Population density decreases with distance from the coast. Each triangle formed by three A-centres contains the same amount of purchasing power.

Figure 9. Distribution of $\underline{A}$ Centres on an Anisotropic Plain

ket areas of suppliers of good $(\underline{n} - \underline{i})$ in the $\underline{A}$ centres, themselves reach the threshold for good $(\underline{n} - \underline{i})$. Good $(\underline{n} - \underline{i})$ will
thus be supplied not only from the $\underline{A}$ centres, but also from a
second set of $\underline{B}$ centres, which appear in the interstices between
the $\underline{A}$ centres and supply good $(\underline{n} - \underline{i})$ and all goods with lower
thresholds.

In order for the $\underline{B}$ centres to be of equal functional complexity, and to be defined by the single hierarchical marginal good
$(\underline{n} - \underline{i})$, it is necessary for the amounts of purchasing power ac-
cumulating in the interstitial areas between the $\underline{A}$ centres to be
in all cases equal or nearly so. If this were not the case, it
would be possible for some goods to be supplied from new interstitial centres before others. This in turn would destroy the
rank structure of the system, since interstitial centres of vary-

ing degrees of functional complexity would spring up as opportunities presented themselves. There would be no "hierarchical marginal goods," since in many cases the marginal good permitting the entry of a new centre would be unique to that particular interstitial area. There would therefore be no definite ranks of centres, and in short, no hierarchy.

Here, then, lies the significance of the statement made above to the effect that all triangles formed by joining neighbouring A centres contain approximately equal amounts of purchasing power. It is this regular feature of a geometrically irregular layout which ensures that interstitial purchasing power accumulates in equal, or nearly equal, amounts; and this, in turn, leads to the quasi-simultaneous appearance of all the B centres, and to the existence of what Berry and Garrison so aptly term a hierarchical marginal good.

This same logic is extended by Berry and Garrison to derive a multi-tiered hierarchy of centres. Successively lower-threshold hierarchical marginal goods duly permit the entry of lower ranks of C centres, D centres, and so forth. The members of each rank occupy the interstices between pre-existing centres of higher rank. A full hierarchy of centres is thus derived without the use of the original Christallerian assumption that disposable income is uniformly distributed.

It is of great importance that this reformulated model of a central place hierarchy is characterized by the same general features as those which were extracted from the Christallerian models for use as diagnostic criteria of hierarchical structuring. In particular, the very existence of hierarchical marginal goods implies that the orders are discretely stratified and distinguished by incremental baskets of goods. It is worth noting, with respect to the Berry and Garrison model, that the accumulations of interstitial purchasing power need not be exactly identical in order for discrete stratification of centres to exist. So long as a hierarchical marginal good is characteristic of the majority of the centres in a given order, and so long as the marginal goods for the other centres in that order have thresholds close to that of the order's hierarchical marginal good, the system will be stratified in the sense that differences in functional complexity between the orders will be greater than differences within the orders. Thus, the criterion of discrete stratification of centrality is inherent not only in the early

Christallerian models, but also in the later and more elegant formulation of Berry and Garrison.

Strictly speaking, the hypothetical stretching of a rubber isotropic plain implies changes not only in the density of purchasing power, but also in the ranges of individual goods. In order for a particular good to retain its identity as the hierarchical marginal good for a particular order, the range of that good must increase along with increases in the distance separating centres of the order in question. As it happens, there is some empirical evidence that the ranges of goods do indeed increase as the density of purchasing power declines.[21] But more important, as noted above, it is not essential to the maintenance of rank structure that one marginal good defines all centres of an order. Thus, even if changes in the ranges of goods do not quite keep pace with changes in the density of purchasing power, it is unlikely that within-rank differences in functional complexity in a single central place system will reach the point where they exceed between-rank differences.

In reformulating Christaller's theory, Berry and Garrison directed their attention only to the Versorgungsprinzip model, in which each order of centres is located at the midpoints of the triangles formed by higher order centres. It is apparent, however, that Berry and Garrison's argument can be extended, with appropriate changes in wording, to cover the Verkehrsprinzip and Absonderungsprinzip models. In the Verkehrsprinzip case, the removal of the assumption that disposable income is uniformly distributed means that each centre, as it is located between two higher-order centres, is not necessarily located exactly half way between the latter. Similarly, in the Absonderungsprinzip case, perfect symmetry in the positioning of interstitial centres is lost. In both cases, as in the Versorgungsprinzip case, geometrical regularity disappears, but the essentials of hierarchical structuring are maintained.

[21]Brian J. L. Berry, Geography of Market Centers and Retail Distribution (Englewood Cliffs, New Jersey: Prentice-Hall, 1967), pp. 32-35.

AN EVALUATION OF
CENTRAL PLACE THEORY

The Löschian Landscape

No review of central place theory is complete without some mention of the work of Lösch. Like Christaller, Lösch assumed an isotropic plain as the basis of his inquiry into the spatial structure of marketing systems. He then postulated that suppliers with hexagonal market areas would locate on this plain in such a way that no excess profits would be earned by the suppliers of any good. [22]

This requirement that all excess profits be eliminated is incompatible with the Christallerian stipulation that the number of central places be minimized, thereby minimizing aggregate consumer travel. In the Christallerian models, suppliers of successively lower-threshold goods locate so far as possible in existing central places, with the result that excess profits are zero only for the suppliers of the hierarchical marginal good of each order. The suppliers of every other good, in order to eliminate their excess profits, would have to ignore the locations of existing central places, and position themselves as close to one another as possible, so as to minimize the size of their market areas. This is precisely the behaviour of suppliers in Lösch's model.

The network of market areas for the suppliers of any one good in the Löschian landscape may be visualized as a fishnet, the size of the mesh being determined by the threshold of the good in question. Since different goods have different thresholds, the complete landscape consists of many such fishnets, each with its own distinctive size of mesh. Lösch postulated that one point on his isotropic plain would by definition be a supply centre for all goods. He then constructed his model by superimposing all possible market area fishnets on the plain, rotating them about the defined central point so that the suppliers of different goods occupied the same locations wherever possible. Note that this attempt to minimize the number of central places was made only after the spacing of each set of sup-

---

[22]August Lösch, The Economics of Location, translated by William H. Woglom and Wolfgang F. Stolper (New Haven: Yale University Press, 1954), pp. 101-137; see also August Lösch, "The Nature of Economic Regions," Southern Economic Journal, Vol. 5 (1938), 71-78.

pliers had been determined in accordance with the requirement that no excess profits be earned.

While Lösch's procedure does create multiple-good supply points, the system is not characterized by incremental baskets of goods. Centres are frequently found which supply goods with large thresholds and goods with small thresholds, but not goods with intermediate thresholds.[23] Moreover, as Johnson has pointed out, Lösch's approach "does not produce the 'tiered' system of urban centres suggested by Christaller."[24] In other words, the system does not exhibit discrete stratification of centrality. On these grounds, one is justified in regarding the Löschian landscape as non-hierarchical.

With real entrepreneurs, a newcomer is more likely to succeed in a place which is already a central place than in an isolated and untried location. In this respect, the Löschian landscape is quite unrealistic, since it incorporates the extreme assumption that the set of firms supplying a particular good locates without any regard whatsoever for the locations already occupied by firms supplying other goods. The great emphasis which Lösch placed on his assumption that no excess profits are earned led him to ignore almost completely the natural agglomerative tendency of central place firms. In the Christallerian models, by contrast, this tendency is given explicit consideration. It is therefore concluded that the Christallerian models are more plausible, and hence heuristically more valuable, than the Löschian landscape.

The tendency of real entrepreneurs to locate in existing central places, rather than in the open countryside, reflects the fact that the population of a central place itself contributes towards the threshold requirements of suppliers locating there. In this connection, the models of Christaller and Lösch are equally open to criticism. Both these writers begin with disposable income uniformly distributed over the isotropic plain, and both proceed to generate landscapes exhibiting population clusters of varying size, which ipso facto negates the basic assumption of uniformly distributed disposable income. Isard has discussed this problem with reference to the Löschian land-

[23]Lösch, The Economics of Location, pp. 124-130.

[24]James H. Johnson, Urban Geography: An Introductory Analysis (Oxford: Pergamon Press, 1967), p. 96.

scape.[25] His solution, in essence, is to shrink the market
areas of large centres and expand those of small centres, on
the grounds that the smaller population of a small centre entails the existence of a larger contingent of rural consumers to
support the supply of a given good. It should be noted that this
solution does not affect the relative functional complexity of the
central places themselves. Hence, the application of a similar
adjustment to the Christallerian models would not destroy their
hierarchical structure.

The Problem of Time

It has occasionally been observed that Christaller's models are
essentially static. They rationalize a state of affairs which is
feasible, but they do not point to any evolutionary process by
which their logical arrangements of central places could have
come about.[26] This comment, of course, can also be applied
to Lösch's work and to the Berry and Garrison model. It is
acknowledged that the formulation of a dynamic model of the
development of a central place network is a formidable problem, and it is probably for this reason that few efforts in this
direction have yet been made.[27] On the other hand, the synoptic feasibility of a model is enough to justify its use as a basis for empirical research. It is valid to inquire whether a
situation which could exist, does exist, even if one has no air-
tight logic to account for its emergence from non-existence or
chaos.

In fact, if logical rigour is not a prime requirement, it is
possible to place dynamic interpretations on the Christaller
and Berry and Garrison models as they stand. Given an initially empty area in which population density steadily increases,
the "process" by which interstitial locations are commandeered
by successively lower ranking centres is not an entirely un-

[25]Walter Isard, Location and Space-Economy (Cambridge: Massachusetts Institute of
Technology Press, 1956), pp. 271-273.

[26]See, for example, James M. Houston, A Social Geography of Europe (London: Duckworth, 1953), p. 141.

[27]The most notable contributions towards a dynamic hierarchical central place model
are the following: James H. Stine, "Temporal Aspects of Tertiary Production Elements
in Korea, " in Urban Systems and Economic Development, edited by Forrest R. Pitts
(Eugene: School of Business Administration, University of Oregon, 1962), pp. 68-88;
Richard L. Morrill, "Simulation of Central Place Patterns over Time, " in Proceedings
of the IGU Symposium in Urban Geography, Lund, 1960, edited by Knut Norborg (Lund:
C. W. K. Gleerup, 1962), pp. 109-120.

realistic one. For example, consider the early decades of European settlement in many parts of the New World. During this period, the first supply points to be established were in general key transportation nodes, and between these nodes lay tracts of land which subsequently were occupied over a more or less extended period of time by a farming population. As settlement proceeded, there would be many opportunities for the commandeering of interstitial locations by new central place entrepreneurs.[28] Older places, which were always older, could grow through time in functional complexity, and thus maintain their positions in the hierarchy. What matters, in other words, is not the absolute commercial status of places, but their relative functional complexity, which in turn is associated with their relative locations. While all places could develop in absolute terms in response to increasing population density, each could still maintain its relative position.[29]

An alternative interpretation, and one which may be more satisfactory from a probabilistic viewpoint, is to regard the development of all central places as controlled, in the last analysis, by the structure of the system of which they are a part. For example, if one assumes the Versorgungsprinzip to be the operative principle in a particular area (or if one has empirical evidence that such is the case), one may contend that the growth of individual places over time must be such that the "climax" or "steady state" pattern of the network conforms to the Versorgungsprinzip model. In other words, one takes the view that the relative spacing and functional complexity of towns results from the operation of Christaller's marketing principle, despite the idiosyncratic "advantages" of individual sites.[30]

[28]As Wade puts it: "The towns were the spearheads of the frontier"; see Richard C. Wade, The Urban Frontier (Cambridge: Harvard University Press, 1959), p. 1. For the case of Ontario, see especially Ontario, Department of Archives, Sixteenth Report, Land Settlement in Upper Canada, 1783-1840, by Gilbert C. Paterson (Toronto: King's Printer, 1921).

[29]This is essentially the conclusion reached by Skinner in his remarks on the growth of market centres in China; see G. William Skinner, "Marketing and Social Structure in Rural China: Part II," Journal of Asian Studies, Vol. 24 (1964-65), 195-202.

[30]This view of the dominant influence of the urban system's structure per se has been voiced in Frederick Lukermann, "Empirical Expressions of Nodality and Hierarchy in a Circulation Manifold," East Lakes Geographer, Vol. 2 (1966), 17-44, especially p. 43.

The Multiple-Good Firm

Turning now to a different problem, it must be noted that each supplier in all the above central place models provides consumers with only one good. Real central place firms, by contrast, rarely deal in just one good. A case could be made that certain service firms, such as barbers and undertakers, come close to being single-good enterprises; but central place firms in general, and especially retailers, provide consumers with a multiplicity of goods. It thus appears that a realistic interpretation of central place theory requires that the multiple-good firm be substituted for the single-good firm as the basic decision-making unit. This implies that the "good" of traditional theory may be thought of as a "package deal," which the relevant entrepreneur habitually considers as a unit when working out his balance sheet or when making a location decision. The realism of this "package deal" view is borne out by the fact that only the most resourceful of prospective proprietors makes any attempt to evaluate potential locations in terms of each separate good in his intended inventory. The important point, however, is that the substitution of the multiple-good firm for the single-good firm entails no alteration in the logical structure of central place models, and hence no change in their distinctive hierarchical characteristics.

It is to be expected that the individual goods supplied by a multiple-good firm have different ranges. Conceivably, therefore, identical multiple-good firms could locate on an isotropic plain at such a distance from one another that they "lose on the roundabouts and gain on the swings." That is to say, they are farther apart than they need to be in order to profit from the sale of goods having low ranges, but too close together to profit from the sale of goods having high ranges. While a break-even equilibrium location pattern for these firms can theoretically be found, it is not likely that in the real world they would accept such a situation. Notwithstanding the proverbial fairground proprietor, it is normal for firms to drop unprofitable lines; the only notable exception to this rule is the practice of attracting customers by deliberately taking a loss on selected goods known as "loss leaders." It may thus be suggested that the distance between multiple-good firms tends to be determined by the highest ranking goods they sell. This tendency, in turn, may be regarded as a basis for specifying the manner in which

42

multiple-good firms locate on the isotropic plain. Again, however, the important point is that the logical structure and distinctive features of central place models remain unaffected by the introduction of the multiple-good firm.

Several conclusions may now be drawn. First, the hierarchical models of Christaller, and of Berry and Garrison, recognize the natural agglomerative tendency of central place firms, and are therefore more plausible than the non-hierarchical Löschian landscape. Secondly, since absolute uniformity in the distribution of disposable income is unlikely to be encountered in reality, the Berry and Garrison model is more plausible than Christaller's original Versorgungsprinzip model. It has also been pointed out that Berry and Garrison's argument can be extended to cover Christaller's Verkehrsprinzip and Absonderungs-prinzip models. Thirdly, although the question of the time element in central place theory is important, the existence of synoptic models is a sufficient basis for inquiring whether real central place systems are hierarchically structured. Fourthly, the realistic concept of the multiple-good firm may be substituted for the traditional fiction of the single-good firm without affecting the hierarchical nature of the Christallerian models.

Finally, empirical studies should be based on criteria of hierarchical structuring which are incontestably grounded in orthodox central place theory. It is contended that the criteria described in this chapter must be employed if the question of the existence of hierarchies of central places is to be satisfactorily answered.

III

Hierarchical Classifications of Towns: a Survey of Past Research

The objective of this chapter is to assess the validity of a number of proposed hierarchical classifications of towns in terms of the characteristics of the ideal hierarchy described above. The works selected for individual treatment are those which have been milestones in their time, or which have provoked important methodological discussions.

EARLY HIERARCHICAL
CLASSIFICATIONS

The first fully articulated hierarchical classification of towns seems to have been that proposed by Kolb on the basis of his work in Wisconsin some forty years ago.[1] Kolb contended that

> . . . no rural community is living up to its opportunity unless attention is being given to at least six fundamental services: the economic, including merchandising, marketing and financing; the educational; the religious; the social; communication and transportation; and that of organization activity itself.[2]

---

[1]Much of Kolb's work was concerned with what he termed the "rural primary group," that is, the first socially significant grouping larger than the family. Kolb's work on Wisconsin, dealing primarily with Dane and Walworth Counties, spanned almost four decades, and is summarized in John H. Kolb, Emerging Rural Communities (Madison: University of Wisconsin Press, 1959).

[2]John H. Kolb, Service Relations of Town and Country, Research Bulletin No. 58 (Madison: University of Wisconsin Agricultural Experiment Station, 1923), p. 3.

Kolb did not expand upon the detailed nature of these services, and it may be questioned whether all of them qualify as central place activities. In particular, "communication and transportation" would appear to be a non-central-place activity, though "communication" probably included the post office, which is certainly a central function. Notwithstanding this reservation, it is instructive to consider the five classes of centres which Kolb proceeded to identify for Wisconsin towns:

(1) the single service type, usually a crossroads store, church, or school;

(2) the limited, simple service type, which at most performs four of the six fundamental services;

(3) the semi-complete or intermediate type, which performs all or all but one of the six;

(4) the complete and partially specialized type, in which the full complement of six services is present, and in which specialized activities (for example, the less common types of retail store), are in evidence;

(5) the urban and highly specialized type, which Kolb notes probably could be subdivided; he includes here both Madison and Milwaukee, but acknowledges their difference in complexity.[3]

Kolb's classification is interesting not only because it was evidently the first attempt at a hierarchical taxonomy to appear, but also because the use of a check-list of index functions to determine a centre's status foreshadows the work of Smailes. The question of immediate concern, however, is whether or not this proposed classification brought about an ordering of towns which would satisfy the basic criteria of hierarchical structuring. Certainly, there are more than two orders in Kolb's scheme, and there is a strong suggestion that the principle of incremental baskets of goods is not violated. On the other hand, since Kolb did not apply his classification explicitly to actual centres, there is no guarantee of spatial interdependence of centres, or of functional wholeness of the system. Moreover, there is no suggestion that the requirements of discrete stratification of centrality and interstitial placement of orders would be met. Thus, Kolb's scheme cannot be said to embody the essential conditions for the existence of an urban hierarchy.

[3]Ibid., pp. 5-7. The classification is also presented in Kolb, Emerging Rural Communities, pp. 102-103.

Many proposed hierarchical classifications of towns turn out, like Kolb's, to be inconclusive because of a lack of attention to the criteria of spatial interdependence, functional wholeness, discrete stratification, and interstitial placement. Kolb himself should not be criticized on this account, for his classificatory proposal was written ten years before Christaller's seminal work on central places appeared, and thirty years before an active interest in central place classifications developed. Nevertheless, it is intriguing that Kolb's proposal falls short of perfection for the same reasons as many much later schemes.

To Arthur Smailes generally goes the credit for the first detailed classification of the central places of an entire national area into hierarchical orders.[4] Dealing with England and Wales, Smailes began by outlining what he considered to be the retail and service attributes of a "fully-fledged town." These attributes were summarized as a list of six index functions: (1) banks, (2) branches of major chain stores (notably Woolworth's), (3) secondary schools, (4) hospitals, (5) cinemas, and (6) weekly newspapers. In order to qualify as a "fully-fledged town," a centre had to possess all of these functions, except that it was permitted to lack either a secondary school or a hospital.

Above this "town" level, Smailes identified three higher orders of central places. At the top came a group of 16 "major cities," including London and such large provincial centres as Birmingham, Manchester, Newcastle, Norwich, and Plymouth. Next came 21 "cities," typified by such places as Northampton, Carlisle, Cambridge, and Exeter; and these were followed by a group of almost 100 "minor cities." Below the "town" level, which itself accounted for some 330 places, Smailes proposed two further orders: "subtowns," which lacked two, three, or four of the basic attributes of "towns" and "urban villages," which possessed at most two of the "town" functions.[5]

Smailes's classification, like that of Kolb, fails to satisfy all the requirements for true hierarchical structuring. To begin with, no evidence is presented that the study area, comprising England and Wales, is a functional whole with respect

---

[4]A classification of Bavarian towns by Christaller predates the work of Smailes by several years, but Christaller is primarily noted for his contribution in the realm of theory. For comments on Christaller's empirical work, see chap. iv below.

[5]Arthur E. Smailes, "The Urban Hierarchy in England and Wales," Geography, Vol. 29 (1944), 41-51.

to central place activities. It might be argued that London performs certain services for the entire area, but there are two objections to this argument. First, the services which London performs for all of England and Wales are not central place services, since they do not influence the everyday behaviour of consumers. People living in the north or the far southwest of England, for example, do not normally have any contact with London for the direct satisfaction of their wants. Secondly, even if non-central-place services performed by London were to be accepted as delimiting a functional whole for a central place study, it may be pointed out that at least Scotland, if not also certain other areas, would have to be added to the study area.

The fact that England and Wales were not shown to constitute a functional whole is not the only reason for doubting the validity of Smailes's classification. Smailes apparently did not consider it necessary to examine his centres for evidence of discrete stratification of centrality. In this connection, he wrote:

Any grading, however, must in some measure be arbitrary, since the urban scale is as continuous as the social scale. Yet the indefiniteness of boundaries in neither case warrants denial of the reality of a stratification.[6]

This is a curious statement in view of the necessary existence of discrete stratification in an ideal hierarchy. Smailes made no attempt to describe how "indefinite" the boundaries were between his various classes of towns, nor to define at what point an indefinite boundary becomes a nonexistent one. The problem here is that, if the boundaries are purely arbitrary, ten researchers working in the same study area might produce ten quite different classifications. In other words, the results are not inevitable, as they would have to be in the case of an ideal hierarchy, but accidental, the break-points between the different orders of centres being chosen at the whim of the individual researcher.

In Smailes's classification, the criteria of incremental baskets of goods, a minimum of three orders, and a pyramid of numbers in order membership are certainly satisfied, but no attention is paid to the criteria of spatial interdependence of

[6]Ibid., 41.

centres, functional wholeness of the system, discrete stratification of centrality, or interstitial placement of orders. An approach similar to that of Smailes, using index functions to designate the status of towns, was used by Dickinson in a study of East Anglia, and also by Duncan, who explicitly adopted Smailes's methodology in his examination of New Zealand centres.[7] All these studies must be regarded as inconclusive with respect to the question of the hierarchical structuring of real central place systems.

LATER CLASSIFICATIONS AND THE RANK-SIZE CONTROVERSY

The first hierarchical classification of central places to appear in the American literature after Smailes's work in Britain was a study of Southwestern Wisconsin by Brush.[8] Brush recognized that there were no clear breaks in population size among the central places in his study area, but he asserted that, in terms of the central functions occurring in these places, "a threefold classification becomes apparent."[9] He proceeded to identify groups of centres termed hamlets, villages, and towns, and to present lists of the functions typically found in each of these orders.

Brush's study was critically examined by Vining, an economist interested in the spatial distribution of cities.[10] In a reprise of the argument for the existence of three orders of centres, Vining emphasized the subjectivity of Brush's classification, and stated that he saw

. . . no evidence . . . for three natural partitions. . . . Like pool, pond, and lake, the terms hamlet, village, and town are convenient modes of expression; but they do not refer to structurally distinct natural entities.[11]

---

[7]Robert E. Dickinson, "The Distribution and Functions of the Smaller Urban Settlements of East Anglia," Geography, Vol. 17 (1932), 19-31; J. S. Duncan, "New Zealand Towns as Service Centres," New Zealand Geographer, Vol. 11 (1955), 119-138.

[8]John E. Brush, "The Hierarchy of Central Places in Southwestern Wisconsin," Geographical Review, Vol. 43 (1953), 380-402.

[9]Ibid., 385.

[10]Rutledge Vining, "A Description of Certain Spatial Aspects of an Economic System," Economic Development and Cultural Change, Vol. 3 (1954-55), 147-195.

[11]Ibid., 169.

Vining went on to argue that towns do not fall into discrete orders, but instead resemble points spaced along a continuum of urban importance. Thus began a debate which continued in the literature until quite recently.

Vining contended that the concept of a hierarchy was incompatible with what has come to be known as the rank-size rule of the distribution of city sizes in a large area. The rank-size rule is an empirical regularity obtained by first ranking by size all the urban centres in a given large area—usually a whole country—and then plotting size against rank on logarithmic graph paper. The points on the graph representing the cities will be found to lie approximately on a straight line, for which the least-squares equation can be calculated by standard regression analysis. This equation is of the form:

$$\text{Log } P_i = \text{Log } P_1 - b. \text{Log } R_i \qquad (1)$$

where P_i and R_i are respectively the size (population), and rank of the i'th largest city, P_1 is the size of the largest city, and $\underline{b}$ is a constant representing the slope of the regression line. This equation may be rewritten as:

$$P_i = P_1 . R_i^{-b} \qquad (2)$$

with the symbols having the same meanings as given above.

The first researcher to observe this regularity in the distribution of city sizes appears to have been Auerbach.[12] Other investigators subsequently found that the rank-size rule was descriptive not only of city sizes, but also of the distribution of incomes by size, of words in written English by frequency of use, and of the output of research papers by scientists.[13] Zipf has drawn these and similar findings together and attempted to formulate a general explanation for them. For the 100 largest cities in the United States in 1940, Zipf found that the exponent $\underline{b}$ in equation (2) above was unity, leading to the rather startling statement that the country's $\underline{n}$'th largest city was $1/\underline{n}$ the size of New York, the largest city. He then suggested that this sim-

[12]Felix Auerbach, "Das Gesetz der Bevölkerungskonzentration," Petermanns Geographische Mitteilungen, Vol. 59, Part 1 (1913), 74-76.

[13]H. W. Singer, "The 'Courbe des Populations': A Parallel to Pareto's Law," Economic Journal, Vol. 46 (1936), 254-263; E. U. Condon, "Statistics of Vocabulary," Science, Vol. 67 (1928), 300; Alfred J. Lotka, "The Frequency Distribution of Scientific Productivity," Journal of the Washington Academy of Sciences, Vol. 16 (1926), 317-323.

plified form of equation (2), having an exponent of unity, was
characteristic of a system (of cities, incomes, words, etc.),
which was "mature" in the sense that the "forces of unification"
and the "forces of diversification" were "in equilibrium."[14]

Thorndike, and later Berry and Garrison, have rightly
pointed out that this proposed explanation is obscure and seem-
ingly devoid of logical foundation, and Stewart has indicated that
data on city sizes for certain countries are fitted more closely
by an S-shaped curve on logarithmic paper than by a straight
line.[15] In addition, Berry has shown that countries with smooth
rank-size distributions of cities do not necessarily have a high
level of economic maturity.[16] Nevertheless, Boal and Johnson
have recently suggested that the rank-size pattern might be used
as a norm or optimum towards which planning programmes
could be directed.[17] It is evident that interpretation of the
meaning of the empirical regularity expressed in the rank-size
rule is still problematical.[18]

When Vining put forward his critique of Brush's study of
Wisconsin central places, he demonstrated that the 157 largest
cities in the United States in 1950 conformed very well to the
rank-size rule. He maintained that if a hierarchy really existed
these centres would form a staircase on the graph rather than a
straight line.[19] Two preliminary points must be made, neither
of which is directly relevant to the main problem, but both of

[14]George K. Zipf, Human Behavior and the Principle of Least Effort (Cambridge: Addison
Wesley Press, 1949), chap. ix; see also George K. Zipf, National Unity and Disunity: The
Nation as a Bio-Social Organism (Bloomington, Indiana: Principia Press, 1941).

[15]E. L. Thorndike, review of Zipf's National Unity and Disunity in Science, Vol. 94
(1941), 19; Brian J. L. Berry and William L. Garrison, "Alternate Explanations of Urban
Rank-Size Relationships," Annals of the Association of American Geographers, Vol. 48
(1958), 83-91; Charles T. Stewart, "The Size and Spacing of Cities," Geographical Review,
Vol. 48 (1958), 222-245.

[16]Brian J. L. Berry, "City Size Distributions and Economic Development," Economic
Development and Cultural Change, Vol. 9 (1961), 573-588.

[17]F. W. Boal and D. B. Johnson, "The Rank-Size Curve: A Diagnostic Tool?" Professional Geographer, Vol. 17, No. 5 (September, 1965), 21-23.

[18]Additional relevant articles include the following: John Q. Stewart, "A Basis for Social
Physics," Impact of Science on Society, Vol. 3 (1952), 110-133; Frederick T. Moore, "A
Note on City Size Distributions," Economic Development and Cultural Change, Vol. 7
(1958-59), 465-466; Kenneth E. Rosing, "A Rejection of the Zipf Model (Rank Size Rule)
in Relation to City Size," Professional Geographer, Vol. 18, No. 2 (March, 1966), 75-82;
Chauncy D. Harris, "City and Region in the Soviet Union," in Urbanization and Its Problems, edited by R. P. Beckinsale and J. M. Houston (Oxford: Basil Blackwell, 1968), pp.
277-296.

[19]Vining, "A Description of Certain Spatial Aspects of an Economic System," 147-152
and 166-171.

which reveal avoidable gaps in Vining's argument. First, only four of the 157 cities considered by Vining lie wholly or partly in Wisconsin (Milwaukee, Duluth-Superior, Madison, and Racine), and not one of these four lies within Brush's study area.[20] Secondly, Vining used population totals to rank his cities, whereas Brush based his classification of centres on their central place functions. For these reasons, one might be inclined to dismiss Vining's case as irrelevant on the grounds that neither the universe of centres analyzed, nor the yardstick of urban importance employed, were comparable with those in Brush's study. On the other hand, these points may be countered by Brush's own admission that there were no clear breaks in the population sizes of his centres, and by the fact that a high positive correlation has been shown to exist between the populations of towns (logarithmically transformed), and the numbers of central functions they perform.[21] In short, there are certainly reasons for questioning the validity of Brush's three orders, and Vining was justified in calling attention to their arbitrary nature.

The problem of reconciling the rank-size rule with the concept of a hierarchy of centres was resolved at the theoretical level by Berry and his associates. In a series of comparative analyses of the central places in several widely separated districts between Chicago and the Rocky Mountains, Berry found that towns containing a given array of central functions varied markedly in population, and this variation depended primarily upon the density of the population in the surrounding area. These findings prompted the realization that an urban hierarchy could exist in which the size and functional complexity of the members of each order changed across space instead of remaining constant. Consider, for example, a large area containing an ideal hierarchy composed of three orders. Variations in population density, or more precisely in the density of disposable income, could result in the size and functional complexity of the centres in the highest order at one side of the area

---

[20]Ibid., 149-151. Compare with Brush, "The Hierarchy of Central Places in Southwestern Wisconsin."

[21]Edwin N. Thomas, "Some Comments on the Functional Bases for Small Iowa Towns," Iowa Business Digest, Vol. 31, No. 2 (February, 1960), 10-16; Howard A. Stafford, "The Functional Bases of Small Towns," Economic Geography, Vol. 39 (1963), 165-175; Brian J. L. Berry, Geography of Market Centers and Retail Distribution (Englewood Cliffs, New Jersey: Prentice-Hall, 1967), pp. 26-40.

resembling the size and functional complexity of the centres in the _middle_ order at the other side of the area. Taking the area as a whole, it might well be found that all values of size and urban centrality were represented, so that in the aggregate there would appear to be a smooth continuum of urban importance from the smallest to the largest centres, and this continuum could well conform to the rank-size rule. Nevertheless, an examination of any one small portion of the area would confirm the existence of a discretely stratified hierarchy of centres.[22]

Thus, reconciliation of the hierarchy concept and the rank-size regularity lies in grasping the distinction between the aggregative and elemental levels of inquiry.[23] A search for a rank-size conformation of centres involves abstracting the centres from their real locations, and ranking them by size regardless of their spatial relationships with one another. A search for a hierarchy, on the other hand, requires that the centres be treated literally _in situ_, that their mutual spatial interrelationships be studied, and that the various other criteria of hierarchical structuring be applied. While the rank-size rule, if indeed it be acceptable as an accurate description of the size distributions of groups of cities, presents problems of interpretation, its existence or nonexistence implies nothing at all about the existence or nonexistence of hierarchical structuring.

While Vining's demonstration that American cities conform to the rank-size rule is thus no proof that hierarchical structuring _cannot_ exist, he was quite correct in stating that evidence of discrete orders _does not_ exist in Brush's study of Wisconsin centres. Not only is there no evidence of discrete stratification among Brush's central places; in addition, there is no suggestion that the centres all belong to the same central place system, or that a complete system is represented. It seems likely, from the locations of the large cities of Madison, La Crosse, and Dubuque just outside the boundary of Brush's study area, that his centres are members of three distinct systems, and

[22]Brian J. L. Berry, H. Gardiner Barnum, and Robert J. Tennant, "Retail Location and Consumer Behavior," _Regional Science Association, Papers and Proceedings_, Vol. 9 (1962), 65-106.

[23]Brian J. L. Berry and H. Gardiner Barnum, "Aggregate Relations and Elemental Components of Central Place Systems," _Journal of Regional Science_, Vol. 4 (1962), 35-68.

that none of these systems is present in its entirety in his study. For several reasons, therefore, Brush's study may be added to the list of works proposing hierarchical classifications which turn out to be inconclusive with regard to demonstrating the existence of a real urban hierarchy. In this respect, Vining's criticisms of Brush, though supported by what is in fact an irrelevant argument woven around the rank-size rule, are in themselves perfectly valid.

PROBLEMS IN GROUPING TECHNIQUE

In a study of part of Snohomish County, Washington, Berry and Garrison expressed their agreement with Vining's judgment on the subjectivity of Brush's classification:

That [Brush] used an arbitrary division and then proved what he had in fact assumed is without question (this criticism applies to more studies of central places than is generally realized).[24]

Berry and Garrison then formulated a more objective classification procedure, from which they argued that evidence of hierarchical structuring among central places did indeed exist.

Berry and Garrison took the numbers of central functions in their centres as the measure of urban centrality, and viewed the centres as points arrayed along a linear scale of increasing centrality. Thus, the numbers of central functions in places were treated as "distance" measurements along a line, and a form of nearest neighbour analysis was applied in order to divide the array of points (places), into groups. Berry and Garrison adopted the convention that a "group" should be a set of points such that each member of the set was closer to some other member of the set than to any point outside that set. This definition was taken from work done in the context of plant ecology by the biologists Clark and Evans.[25] Applying this definition of "group" to their centrality measurements, Berry and Garrison identified a three-order hierarchy of centres in their study area.

---

[24]Brian J. L. Berry and William L. Garrison, "The Functional Bases of the Central Place Hierarchy," Economic Geography, Vol. 34 (1958), 146.

[25]Philip J. Clark and Francis C. Evans, "Distance to Nearest Neighbor as a Measure of Spatial Relationships in Populations," Ecology, Vol. 35 (1954), 445–453.

Berry and Garrison grouped not only the places in Snohomish County; they also grouped the functions on the basis of their threshold populations. The threshold was operationally defined as the minimum number of people required in a town to support the performance of a given central function. A graph was prepared for each function in the study area. Each point on these graphs represented a central place, the axes being scaled to show the population of the place, P, and the number of establishments, N, which it contained of the function in question. Best-fitting least-squares curves of the exponential family $P = A.B^N$ were then fitted to the graphs (A and B being constants for each curve), and the threshold of each function was taken as the value of P where $N = 1$. Berry and Garrison then regarded these threshold values as points spaced along a scale of population size, and, again using the Clark and Evans definition of a group, divided the array of functions into three classes. Finally, analysis of variance was used to show that these three groups of functions corresponded to, and were diagnostic of, the three orders of central places already identified.

Because both the places and the functions were grouped into orders, and because a consistent definition of "group" was applied in each case, the results of this Snohomish County study seem to be more conclusive than is actually the case. By experimenting with an arbitrary array of points along a line, one soon discovers that the number of groups which can be identified using the Clark and Evans definition is limited only by the extent to which the researcher wishes to carry the analysis. This fact was recognized by King, who painstakingly duplicated Berry and Garrison's study design in his investigation of the central places of Canterbury, New Zealand:

On the theoretical level two major criticisms can be levelled at the study. The first concerns the method of grouping and the determination of a hierarchical structure. This criticism may be discussed with reference to the grouping of functions although it applies equally as well to the grouping of towns. The threshold populations are treated as points on a line continuum and a group is defined as a set of points each of which is closer to some other member of the group than to some point outside the group. The question arises as to how many groups are to be recognized. . . . Certainly with respect to the list of functions for Canterbury, additional divisions . . . could be defended. The Snohomish County studies should not be regarded as inviolable on this point. The three groupings used by Berry and Garrison could also be broken down into a far larger number. [26]

[26]Leslie J. King, "The Functional Role of Small Towns in Canterbury," Proceedings of the Third New Zealand Geography Conference (Palmerston North: New Zealand Geographical Society, 1961), p. 147.

54

In other words, the number of orders of functions (or of central places), identified by this method is ultimately governed by the point at which the researcher decides to cease applying the grouping technique. The determination of this point is clearly not a part of the grouping technique as such, and must presumably be arrived at subjectively. In that it recognized the need for greater objectivity in research, Berry and Garrison's study of Snohomish County represented a significant advance over previous central place studies. However, the equivocal nature of the grouping technique necessitates the suspension of judgment as to whether the study conclusively demonstrated the existence of a real hierarchy of central places.

The problematical element in this discussion is the Clark and Evans definition of "group." This definition, which bears repeating, is that a group is a set of points such that each member of the set is closer to some other member than to any point outside that set. The important phrase in this definition is "closer to some other member." For the case of an ideal hierarchy, with fully discrete levels of centrality, the definition of a group would have to be: a set of points such that each member of the set is closer to all other members than to any point outside that set. The distinction between "some" and "all" here is critical, since only the use of "all" guarantees that differences in centrality within any one group will be less than the differences between that group and adjacent groups. Inspected on the basis of this modified definition, Berry and Garrison's Snohomish County data yield no groupings whatsoever.

It may be objected that insistence on between-group differences being greater than within-group differences represents too extreme a position. The real world, after all, is a complex place, and flexibility rather than rigidity of approach is desirable. There is value in this latter view, but the Clark and Evans criterion for grouping goes too far. One can visualize a situation in which central places do tend to cluster around certain values of centrality, even though between-group differences are less than within-group differences, and such a case would certainly be accepted as evidence of a hierarchy. What is needed is a grouping technique which is sufficiently flexible to allow the identification of hierarchical tendencies falling short of perfection, yet which is not as permissive, and hence inconclusive, as the Clark and Evans method. An attempt is made in chapter iv to design a technique which meets these specifications.

In a more recent study, carried out in Southwestern Iowa, Berry and his associates adopted a different approach to the problem of grouping central places and central functions into orders.[27] They first summarized the occurrence of central functions in their study area by preparing an incidence matrix in which the rows were central places and the columns were central functions. Cells in this matrix were coded 1 if a function was present in a centre, and zero otherwise. The matrix was then subjected to direct factor analysis, from which it was concluded that the study area contained three orders of central places and three orders of central functions associated with them.[28] These three orders were then shown as points on a graph in which the abscissa was the number of central functions in places, and the ordinate was the logarithm of the number of functional units in places; a functional unit was equivalent to a single establishment except that an establishment performing two distinct functions (for example, furniture sales and under-taking), was counted as two separate functional units.

A noteworthy feature of this graph, which is reproduced as Figure 10, is that it shows a smooth continuum of centres from the smallest "village" to the largest "city," yet it has been divided into three orders. Further, Berry asserts that there are breaks in functional complexity between these orders, and that each order forms a "regime" with its own distinctive slope on the graph.[29] It has been noted earlier, in discussing the rank-size rule, that it is theoretically possible for the orders in a hierarchy to change in centrality across space, and hence the existence of a smooth curve like that in Figure 10 does not, by itself, disprove the existence of hierarchical structuring. On the other hand, the reality of a hierarchy remains in doubt unless the method of classification explicitly incorporates a consideration of the disposition of the centres on the ground. In the study under review, no attempt was made to identify a spa-

[27]Berry, Barnum, and Tennant, "Retail Location and Consumer Behavior."

[28]A fourth order, lower than the other three, was also identified, but this fourth order was excluded from the subsequent stages of the analysis. For a discussion of direct factor analysis, see Brian J. L. Berry, "Grouping and Regionalizing: An Approach to the Problem Using Multivariate Analysis," in Quantitative Geography: Part I: Economic and Cultural Topics, edited by William L. Garrison and Duane F. Marble, Northwestern University Studies in Geography No. 13 (Evanston, Illinois: Department of Geography, Northwestern University, 1967), pp. 219-251.

[29]Berry, Barnum, and Tennant, "Retail Location and Consumer Behavior," fig. 7, p. 7

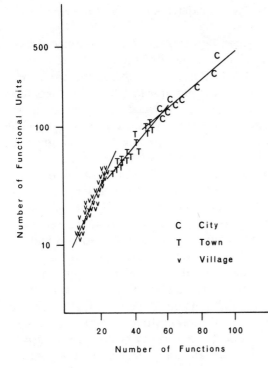

Figure 10. Classification of Central Places
in Part of Iowa (after Berry). By permission,
Regional Science Association, Papers, IX
(1962).

tial system of central places, or to apply the criterion of interstitial placement of orders. The centres were indeed mapped,
and comments were made concerning their pattern of location,
but the mapping was carried out only after the centres had been
classified by factor analysis of the original data matrix. In
short, the best fitting "regimes" shown on Figure 10 refer to
an aggregate of data abstracted from location, and there is
thus no guarantee that the classification of any particular centre has significance in a spatial context.

This particular form of the grouping problem reappears in
recent studies of the central places of Tasmania by Scott.
Scott's work is worthy of comment because it does not stop with
formulating a classification of centres, but goes on to discuss
each order's distribution pattern, and examines the relation-

ships of the latter with physiography, settlement history, and types of farming.[30]

Like Berry, Scott began by making a full inventory of the central functions in the places in his study area. He did not subject these data to factor analysis, but instead plotted them directly on to a graph of central functions against the logarithm of functional units.[31] He then asserted that the curvilinear array of points on the graph fell naturally into three groups, each group exhibiting a distinctive rectilinear regime. The groups thus identified were subjected individually to linear regression analysis, and it was found that the coefficient of linear correlation between functions and the logarithms of functional units exceeded 0.95 for each of the three regimes. The regimes were then designated hamlets, villages, and towns respectively.

Scott's technique, as Johnston has shown in a brief and brilliant paper, amounted to no more than an exercise in self-delusion.[32] Johnston pointed out that by no stretch of the imagination could clusters of points be identified on Scott's graph, and he also noted that the high correlation coefficients resulted simply from the fact that the three rectilinear regimes identified by Scott reduced the curvilinear array of points to segments which were approximately straight lines. By using ten regimes, instead of only three, to approximate the curve, coefficients as high as 0.99 might have been obtained.[33] Johnston made it clear that the selection of rectilinear regimes to approximate a curvilinear array is, in the absence of natural breaks in the distribution of the points, an entirely subjective process. He expressed the possibility that Scott's selection may have been influenced by the optical impression of changes in slope occasioned by the alteration in the spacing of the printed lines at each phase change (4, 10, 40, 100, and so forth), on standard

---

[30]Peter Scott, "The Hierarchy of Central Places in Tasmania," Australian Geographer, Vol. 9 (1964-65), 134-147; also his "Areal Variations in the Class Structure of the Central-Place Hierarchy," Australian Geographical Studies, Vol. 2 (1964), 73-86. Other investigators before Scott have made isolated comments on the relationships between the class structure of proposed hierarchies and such factors as relief and drainage, but Scott was the first to make these relationships the subject of a separate study.

[31]Scott's definition of a "functional unit" differed slightly from that used by Berry, but the difference is not sufficient to warrant special attention.

[32]R. J. Johnston, "The Measurement of a Hierarchy of Central Places," Australian Geographer, Vol. 9 (1964-65), 315-317.

[33]Since Scott did not factor analyze his data, it may be noted that his selection of three regimes lacked even the statistical authenticity of Berry's work on Iowa.

semi-logarithmic graph paper. Whether for this reason or not, it is abundantly clear from Johnston's analysis that Scott's three orders of central places were defined by a completely arbitrary procedure. The classification could scarcely be less inevitable. To all of this, Scott's only reply was that the regimes he had chosen were supported by "other evidence" (not given), and that "all central place classifications are to a greater or lesser extent arbitrary."[34] This latter statement, as the present survey attempts to show, is an accurate description of the facts, but it completely begs one of the principal questions in central place research.

A direct implication of Johnston's criticism of Scott is that the latter's comments on the relationships between the classes in his hierarchy and such factors as relief and types of farming are unproductive of generalized conclusions, since they are the accidental results of an arbitrary classification of centres. A different researcher, in other words, might choose to see four orders of centres, or five, or only two, where Scott saw three, with the result that the distribution patterns of the various orders would show different relationships with physiography and other factors. One cannot usefully discuss areal variations in an urban hierarchy unless the hierarchy itself incontestably exists.

The American studies directed by Berry, and the work of Scott in Tasmania, fail to provide conclusive evidence of the reality of hierarchical structuring. Their failure is due partly to the fact that discrete stratification of centrality is not shown to exist, but equally to the fact that no attention is paid to the spatial aspects of the hierarchy concept. Nowhere in these studies is there any suggestion that the centres analyzed are all members of the same central place system, or that all members of a particular system have been included in the analysis. Yet the identification of a complete system must necessarily precede any tests for stratification if the question of the existence of an urban hierarchy is to be satisfactorily answered.

---

[34]Peter Scott, "The Measurement of a Hierarchy of Central Places: A Reply, " Australian Geographer, Vol. ·9 (1964-65), 317-318.

Hierarchical classifications of central places proposed by previous researchers fail to satisfy the basic criteria of hierarchical structuring derived from central place theory. In particular, the criteria of spatial interdependence of centres, functional wholeness of the central place system, discrete stratification of centrality, and interstitial placement of orders, are not given proper attention. The studies treated individually above were selected from a longer list of works, all of which exhibited the same shortcomings. This list includes studies carried out by Bracey, Carruthers, Fullerton, Lomas, and Carter in Britain;[35] by Hoffer and Borchert in the United States;[36] by Woroby and Thoman in Canada;[37] by Melvin and Grove in West Africa;[38] by Ullman in the Philippine Islands;[39] by Kar and Mayfield in India;[40]

[35]Howard E. Bracey, "A Rural Component of Centrality Applied to Six Southern Counties in the United Kingdom, " Economic Geography, Vol. 32 (1956), 38-50; also his "English Central Villages: Identification, Distribution and Functions, " in Proceedings of the IGU Symposium in Urban Geography, Lund, 1960, edited by Knut Norborg (Lund: C. W. K. Gleerup, 1962), pp. 169-190; I. Carruthers, "A Classification of Service Centres in England and Wales, " Geographical Journal, Vol. 123 (1957), 371-385; B. Fullerton, The Pattern of Service Industries in Northeast England, Department of Geography Research Series No. 3 (Newcastle upon Tyne: Department of Geography, King's College, University of Durham, 1960); G. M. Lomas, "Retail Trading Centres in the Midlands, " Journal of the Town Planning Institute, Vol. 50 (1964), 104-119; Harold Carter, The Towns of Wales: A Study in Urban Geography (Cardiff: University of Wales Press, 1965), chap. vi.

[36]Charles R. Hoffer, "The Changing Ecological Pattern in Rural Life, " Rural Sociology, Vol. 13 (1948), 176-180; John R. Borchert and Russell B. Adams, Trade Centers and Trade Areas of the Upper Midwest, Urban Report No. 3 (Minneapolis: Upper Midwest Research and Development Council, 1963).

[37]P. Woroby, "Functional Ranks and Locational Patterns of Service Centres in Saskatchewan" (abstract), Canadian Geographer, No. 14 (1959), 43; internal evidence indicates that Woroby also was the principal author of: Saskatchewan, Royal Commission on Agriculture and Rural Life, Report No. 12, Service Centers (Regina: Queen's Printer, 1957); Richard S. Thoman and Maurice H. Yeates, Delimitation of Development Regions in Canada (With Special Attention to the Georgian Bay Vicinity) (Ottawa: Area Development Agency, Department of Industry. 1966).

[38]Ernest E. Melvin, "Native Urbanism in West Africa, " Journal of Geography, Vol. 60 (1961), 9-16; David Grove and Laszlo Huszar, The Towns of Ghana: The Role of Service Centres in Regional Planning (Accra: Ghana Universities Press, 1964).

[39]Edward L. Ullman, "Trade Centers and Tributary Areas of the Philippines, " Geographical Review, Vol. 50 (1960), 203-218.

[40]N. R. Kar, "Urban Hierarchy and Central Functions around Calcutta in Lower West Bengal, India, and Their Significance, " in Proceedings of the IGU Symposium in Urban Geography, Lund, 1960, edited by Knut Norborg (Lund: C. W. K. Gleerup, 1962), pp. 253-274; Robert C. Mayfield, "A Central-Place Hierarchy in Northern India, " in Quantitative Geography: Part I: Economic and Cultural Topics, edited by William L. Garrison and Duane F. Marble, Northwestern University Studies in Geography No. 13 (Evanston, Illinois: Department of Geography, Northwestern University, 1967), pp. 120-166.

by Chilczuk in Poland;[41] by Barnum in West Germany;[42] and by Palomäki in Finland.[43] All these studies develop hierarchical classifications which on close examination are seen to be arbitrary rather than inevitable. The general conclusion is that the question of the existence of hierarchical structuring is left unanswered by these writers.

There are several instances of two or more researchers producing hierarchical classifications for the same area. In all these cases, the studies concerned differ widely in their results, a situation which could not occur if the results were inevitable. One example is provided by the works of Smailes, Green, and Carruthers on England and Wales.[44] Considerable differences exist between these classifications, and more than one observer has noted this fact. Thus Berry, commenting on these British studies, wrote:

One wonders about the value of continued a priori allocation of towns to classes, details of the hierarchy existing by definition alone, when one sees the typical 20 percent disagreement between classifications.[45]

Similar reservations have been expressed by Lipman and, more recently, by Murphy and Davies.[46]

Not all the examples of mutual disagreement in identifying classes of central places are found among studies of British towns. Chabot has presented a map showing the tributary areas

[41]M. Chilczuk, "Functions and Dynamics of Transitional Type Settlements in Poland," Geographia Polonica, Vol. 2 (1964), 133-138. The main part of Chilczuk's work is available only in Polish, but is reviewed briefly in Leszek Kosinski, "Population and Urban Geography in Poland," Geographia Polonica, Vol. 1 (1964), 79-96; and in Maria Kielczewska-Zaleska, "Geographical Studies on Rural Settlement in Poland," Geographia Polonica, Vol. 1 (1964), 97-110.

[42]H. Gardiner Barnum, Market Centers and Hinterlands in Baden-Württemberg, Department of Geography Research Paper No. 103 (Chicago: Department of Geography, University of Chicago, 1966).

[43]Mauri Palomäki, "The Functional Centers and Areas of South Bothnia, Finland," Fennia, Vol. 88, No. 1 (1964), 1-235.

[44]Smailes, "The Urban Hierarchy in England and Wales"; F. H. W. Green, "Urban Hinterlands in England and Wales: An Analysis of Bus Services," Geographical Journal, Vol. 116 (1950), 64-81; Carruthers, "A Classification of Service Centres in England and Wales."

[45]Brian J. L. Berry, "Recent Studies Concerning the Role of Transportation in the Space Economy," Annals of the Association of American Geographers, Vol. 49 (1959), 339, footnote.

[46]V. D. Lipman, "Town and Country: The Study of Service Centres and Their Areas of Influence," Public Administration, Vol. 30 (1952), 210-211; Raymond E. Murphy, The American City: An Urban Geography (New York: McGraw-Hill, 1966), pp. 91-93; Wayne K. D. Davies, "The Ranking of Service Centres: A Critical Review," Institute of British Geographers, Transactions, No. 40 (1966), 51-65.

of les grandes villes françaises, the latter being a set of cities
which are mutually competitive and therefore represent centres
above a certain level in an implicit hierarchy.[47] These centres
do not correspond to the cities above any one of the levels in
Coppolani's hierarchical classification of French towns.[48] For
example, south of a line from the Gironde estuary through
Limoges to Lake Geneva, Chabot's grandes villes are 18 in number, while the closest possible correspondence with Coppolani's
classification yields 13 cities of rank sous-capital or higher.
At a more local scale, there is disagreement between Coppolani'
classification as it applies to the Département of Gers in
Aquitaine, and Kendall's early classification of the central places
of this area.[49]

Perhaps the outstanding case among all examples of this
type of disagreement is that between the works of Berry and
Borchert covering an area in northeastern South Dakota. In
this area, five of the six orders identified by Borchert for the
whole Upper Midwest are present, and Berry likewise recognizes five levels of central places. The similarity, however,
ceases at that point. Borchert's three highest orders collapse
to two in Berry's study. For the next lower order, the two
studies together include ten places, but have only five in common. For the next order, Borchert's lowest, the corresponding figures are 31 and 20; and finally, Berry's lowest order of
20 centres contains 16 places which do not appear at all in
Borchert's study. Both studies, it should be noted, set out to
be comprehensive in their coverage of central places, and both
sought to identify a meaningful hierarchy, yet the above comparison is the closest that can be accomplished by juggling the
various orders in the two schemes.[50]

[47]Georges Chabot, "Présentation d'une Carte des Zones d'Influence des Grandes Villes
Françaises, " in Proceedings of the IGU Symposium in Urban Geography, Lund, 1960,
edited by Knut Norborg (Lund: C. W. K. Gleerup, 1962), pp. 197-199.

[48]Jean Coppolani, Le Réseau Urbain de la France: Sa Structure et Son Aménagement
(Paris: Editions Ouvrières, 1959).

[49]H. M. Kendall, "Fairs and Markets in the Department of Gers, France, " Economic
Geography, Vol. 12 (1936), 351-358.

[50]Borchert and Adams, Trade Centers and Trade Areas of the Upper Midwest. Berry's
work on northeastern South Dakota has not been published in full, but a truncated version
of one of the relevant maps appears in his Geography of Market Centers and Retail Distribution, p. 31.

If central place studies were carried out in a manner which involved the consistent application of the criteria of an ideal hierarchy, it would not be possible for such large differences in the conclusions of separate investigators to occur. That these differences occur is not proof that hierarchical structuring is absent from the areas studied, but it does indicate that the researchers concerned have proceeded in a fashion which begs the question. Moreover, as long as hierarchical classifications depend upon the whim of the individual, comparisons between studies carried out in different areas are quite meaningless. The chief example to date of this type of comparison has been provided by Brush and Bracey, who collaborated on an article in which the former's study of Southwestern Wisconsin was compared with the latter's analysis of an area in Southern England. The central argument of this article is worth quoting in full:

Comparative analysis of the distribution of rural service centers in southwestern Wisconsin and southern England shows that the spatial patterns are alike. Though the two areas are unlike in population density, urbanization, and transportation and though there are profound differences in settlement history, two orders of service centers exist in both, spaced at about 21-mile and 8- or 10-mile intervals. A third, and still lower, order, spaced at 4- to 6-mile intervals, also appears in both areas. It is impossible to equate the functional importance of rural service centers in Wisconsin and England because of economic and cultural differences. Indeed, distinctive functional types of centers should exist in every major economic or cultural realm on earth. But the similarities in distribution pattern in Wisconsin and England suggest that there are certain common spatial relationships in the hierarchy of rural service centers.[51]

Since the hierarchical classifications produced separately by Brush and Bracey were in fact arbitrary, it follows that the typical spacings recorded for their various orders of centres are in no sense fundamental properties of the urban networks examined. Thus, instead of arguing that "there are certain common spatial relationships in the hierarchy of rural service centers," it is more correct to say that Brush and Bracey stumbled on the fact that their separate, arbitrary classifications gave rise to typical spacings which, quite fortuitously, happened to be the same in the two cases. In fact, one could take

---

[51]John E. Brush and Howard E. Bracey, "Rural Service Centers in Southwestern Wisconsin and Southern England," Geographical Review, Vol. 45 (1955), 559.

<u>any</u> two study areas, and deliberately classify the central places found there into groups so that the typical spacings in the groups would correspond in the two areas. All this is not to deny that there may be regularities in the spacing of orders in central place hierarchies in different areas. It is merely to point out that such regularities should not be sought unless the hierarchies themselves truly exist.

THE SPATIAL DIMENSION

In a recent review of the type of study in which towns are classified according to their dominant or distinctive economic activities, Smith concluded that

. . . specific geographic objectives—or, for that matter, objectives in general—usually are difficult to discern in the statements of purpose appearing in functional classifications of towns.[52]

Smith's comment applies with equal force to central place classifications. A central place hierarchy, if it exists in the real world, is an explicitly geographic phenomenon, since it represents a spatial ordering of consumer servicing activities. Consequently, any study which ignores the spatial linkages existing among central places is by definition incapable of demonstrating whether a hierarchy exists or not. Yet the criterion of the spatial interdependence of centres has been ignored in the studies so far examined.[53]

In addition, previous researchers have avoided the criteria of discrete stratification of centrality and interstitial placement of orders. While perfect discreteness would require that differences among the members of a given order be less than the differences between that order and neighbouring orders, one can visualize a partial or imperfect hierarchy in which breaks in functional complexity are not so clearly marked. However, studies abound in which there is not the slightest evidence of any breaks at all. The conclusion, to quote again from Vining,

[52]Robert H. T. Smith, "Method and Purpose in Functional Town Classification, " <u>Annals of the Association of American Geographers</u>, Vol. 55 (1965), 539.

[53]One study which does take intercentre linkages into account, but which is concerned with a communications network rather than a central place system, is John D. Nystuen and Michael F. Dacey, "A Graph Theory Interpretation of Nodal Regions, " <u>Regional Science Association, Papers and Proceedings</u>, Vol. 7 (1961), 29-42.

must be that "the number of types or classes into which cities are classified, and the definitions of these classes, are arbitrary."[54] This would not be so if studies had been designed to incorporate the criteria of spatial interdependence of centres, functional wholeness of the system, discrete stratification of centrality, and interstitial placement of orders.

Apart from those who have written of the conflicting results obtained by different investigators in the same area, two writers have commented in general terms upon the inadequacies of past hierarchical classifications of towns, though without making explicit the reasons for these inadequacies. Thus Trotier has stated that

> . . . if hierarchies do exist among the cities of an urban network, this means that there are categories of cities in the various activities; that is, cities of a first order, second order, etc., could be defined, and every city would belong to one of these categories. In other words, there would not be a continuum among cities, from the least important to the most important in every activity, but groupings of cities about certain values and nothing between the groupings. Many authors have thus proposed a terminology for these types of service centres that were said to exist. Actually, it was never empirically proved that such hierarchies do exist.[55]

And these sentiments are echoed and expanded by Snyder:

> There is little uniformity of purpose among the works in the literature that have dealt with questions of urban place patterns. Attempts to synthesize these findings are encumbered by lack of comparability. . . . The concept of a hierarchy of urban places functions as an exceedingly useful, though somewhat arbitrary, analytical tool. In this respect the use of a system of types, or classes, or levels, of urban places is not unlike the regional concept as promulgated by geographers. . . . Neither the regions nor the urban classes do, in fact, exist in other than arbitrary form. . . . Even the use of impersonal statistical mechanisms does not divorce the resultant classification, or areal differentiation, from the initial assumptions of the statistical manipulator.[56]

If indeed it were true that central place hierarchies could exist in none other than arbitrary form, one could do little more than enter a plea that a simple and consistent classification be adopted henceforth as a matter of convention. One recent study, however, has shown that a perfect hierarchy of central places

[54]Vining, "A Description of Certain Spatial Aspects of an Economic System," 165.

[55]Louis Trotier, "Some Functional Characteristics of the Main Service Centres of the Province of Quebec," Cahiers de Géographie de Québec, No. 6 (1959), 253.

[56]David E. Snyder, "Urban Places in Uruguay and the Concept of a Hierarchy," in Festschrift: Clarence F. Jones, edited by Merle C. Prunty, Northwestern University Studies in Geography No. 6 (Evanston, Illinois: Department of Geography, Northwestern University, 1962), pp. 29-30.

undoubtedly existed in Southern China prior to, and possibly since, the 1949 Communist Revolution. Skinner, the anthropologist who carried out this study, did not explicitly itemize the criteria of hierarchical structuring here enumerated, but they are none the less built into his methodology.[57]

In Skinner's study, spatial linkages between central places are represented by the movements of buyers and sellers throughout a given marketing system, the latter achieving its identity as a set of market centres of various sizes tributary to a selected "central market town." In several examples of such systems investigated by Skinner, discrete stratification of centres was shown in three ways: first, by clear differences in the inventories of goods offered by centres at different levels; secondly, by equally clear breaks in the population sizes of the centres; and thirdly, by the fact that official market days in successively higher orders occurred with increasing frequency. It is of paramount significance that Skinner addressed the question of stratification only after he had demonstrated the existence of a system of market centres.

Skinner's work also takes account of the criterion of interstitial placement of orders. In fact, the marketing systems which he investigated are shown to conform to the model layouts depicted in Figures 5 and 7. Skinner thus became the first and only researcher conclusively to demonstrate the reality of a spatial hierarchy of central places.[58]

The failure of so many previous writers to give adequate thought to the fundamental criteria of hierarchical structuring is somewhat puzzling, but there can be little doubt that this failure reflects a lack of understanding of the work of central place theorists. The preceding chapter has shown that orthodox central place theory can be used as a basis for the formulation of diagnostic criteria of hierarchical structuring, and it has been argued that these criteria must be applied in empirical studies if the question of the existence of hierarchies of central places is to be satisfactorily answered. Previous studies have in general failed to apply these criteria, and have therefore failed to answer this question. An immediate need in central

---

[57]G. William Skinner, "Marketing and Social Structure in Rural China: Part I," Journal of Asian Studies, Vol. 24 (1964-65), 3-43.

[58]Ibid., especially the diagrams on pp. 22, 23, 25, 26, and 28.

place research is the translation of the basic criteria of hierarchical structuring into operational terms for use in empirical work.

IV

The Design of Empirical Studies

This chapter represents the link between theory and empirical work. Its purpose is to lay down procedures for the investigation of real central place networks, and, in particular, to render operational the criteria of hierarchical structuring previously described. A valid set of empirical techniques, soundly based in theory and consistently applied to the real world, is a necessary prerequisite for significant progress in central place research. In attempting to set forth such techniques, this chapter seeks to accomplish the single most important objective of the present study.

IDENTIFICATION OF
SYSTEMS OF CENTRES

Limitations of Traditional Techniques
Before an array of central places can be deemed hierarchical or otherwise, it is necessary to ensure that all centres in the array are members of the same central place system, and also that all members of the system in question are included in the analysis. In principle, the delimitation of a town's umland is sufficient to identify the limits of its central place system. However, it must be emphasized that it is not the trace of the umland boundary which gives identity to the system of central places. Rather, the boundary is simply a reflection of the areal extent of the intercentre ties of dependency which hold the system together. It is these intercentre linkages that are the

true cement in the structure of the system. Therefore, a town's umland only identifies a complete central place system if it is delimited in a manner which takes into account the actual spatial interdependencies among central places.

An examination of existing techniques of umland delimitation shows that in general they fail to incorporate explicit consideration of intercentre linkages. Consider, for example, the familiar gravity model technique, originally developed by Reilly.[1] When used as a predictive model to identify the point of consumer indifference between two competing centres, this technique employs only data on the magnitudes of the centres and the distance between them, and does not consider actual movements of people and goods. In addition, writers on retail gravitation have not been able to lay down specific rules governing the researcher's choice of centres which compete with each other and thereby limit the extent of each other's umlands. The model cannot be applied without the prior identification of mutually competitive centres, but the arbitrary and subjective selection of such centres gives no guarantee that a true delimitation of any one centre's umland will be obtained. Suppose the task is to find, with the aid of the gravity model, the western limit of the umland of Toronto. Which other city is the right one to use in the model? Hamilton? London? Detroit? Examples of this kind of uncertainty could readily be multiplied. The essential point is that the gravity model technique does not take account of the actual intercentre linkages among towns, and therefore it is unreliable as a method of identifying complete systems of central places.

The problem of selecting mutually competitive centres is by no means confined to studies employing the gravity model. Consider the method of delimiting umlands through analysis of newspaper circulation data, as originally proposed by Park.[2] In this

[1]William J. Reilly, Methods for the Study of Retail Relationships, Studies in Marketing No. 4 (Austin: Bureau of Business Research, University of Texas, 1959; a reprint of the 1929 edition); William J. Reilly, The Law of Retail Gravitation (New York: By the author, 1931). The following are also useful: Frank Strohkarck and Katherine Phelps, "The Mechanics of Constructing a Market Area Map," Journal of Marketing, Vol. 12 (1947–48), 493–496; George Schwartz, "Laws of Retail Gravitation: An Appraisal," University of Washington Business Review, Vol. 22, No. 1 (October, 1962), 53–70.

[2]Robert E. Park, "Urbanization as Measured by Newspaper Circulation," American Journal of Sociology, Vol. 35 (1929), 60–79. For more recent examples, see the following: J. P. Haughton, "Local Newspapers and the Regional Geographer," Advancement of Science, Vol. 7 (1950), 44–45; Marcel Gauchy, "Le Rayonnement des Journaux Toulousains,"

method, the problem is implicitly solved by defining the universe of mutually competitive centres to include only those towns which publish daily newspapers. It is true that there is evidence to support the view that the umland of a town is closely reflected by the sphere of dominance of its daily newspaper, and it may well be that this method of umland delimitation is more reliable than alternative available techniques.[3] On the other hand, there is a very real possibility that the umlands of some centres which publish daily newspapers are limited in extent partly by the influence of centres which do not publish daily newspapers. In such cases, the practice of considering only newspaper towns would give inaccurate results. Moreover, since the method can be applied only to towns which are large enough to publish a daily newspaper, it lacks the generality which is required if central places of all sizes are to be studied.

The same problem recurs in Green's technique of analyzing the timetables of scheduled bus services.[4] Here, the universe of mutually competitive centres is defined to include every town which is the terminus of a regularly scheduled bus route serving no centre larger than the terminal town. This definition has the effect of placing many small English market towns on an equal competitive footing with metropolitan giants like Birmingham and Manchester. As a result, large centres like the latter are given diminutive umlands which are quite meaningful as a reflection of local bus routes, but which do not take into account the influence of such centres above and beyond the local level.[5] The method is therefore unsuitable as a means of identifying the central place systems of large towns. In addition, the method is inappropriate in North America, where many areas have no

Revue Géographique des Pyrénées et du Sud-Ouest, Vol. 26 (1955), 100-112; Abel Chatelain, "Géographie Sociologique de la Presse et Régions Françaises," Revue de Géographie de Lyon, Vol. 32 (1957), 127-134.

[3]Robert E. Park and Charles Newcomb, "Newspaper Circulation and Metropolitan Regions," contributed in Roderick D. McKenzie, The Metropolitan Community (New York: McGraw-Hill, 1933), pp. 98-110; Arthur E. Smailes, "The Analysis and Delimitation of Urban Fields," Geography, Vol. 32 (1947), 151-161.

[4]F. H. W. Green, "Urban Hinterlands in England and Wales: An Analysis of Bus Services,' Geographical Journal, Vol. 116 (1950), 64-81; also his "Community of Interest Areas: Notes on the Hierarchy of Central Places and Their Hinterlands," Economic Geography, Vol. 34 (1958), 210-226.

[5]None of Green's published articles includes a map of his bus umlands for the whole of Great Britain. However, the complete map was published in 1954 by the British Ordnance Survey as two sheets at 1:625,000, entitled Local Accessibility. Also of interest are the comments in V. D. Lipman, "Town and Country: The Study of Service Centres and Their Areas of Influence," Public Administration, Vol. 30 (1952), 203-214.

bus service and where virtually all shopping trips are made by automobile.

In several studies, the umlands of individual towns have been delimited on the basis of interviews carried out with the merchants in the town or with the consumers in the countryside. Representative examples of this type of study include works by Dickinson, Cassady and Ostlund, Deasy, and the University of Iowa's Bureau of Business and Economic Research.[6] Typically, these studies delimit separate tributary areas for a variety of particular goods and services, and conclude by drawing a single umland boundary which does a minimum of injustice to a maximum number of merchants. In the context of the present study, this approach is more promising than those discussed above, since only a technique involving interviews can directly identify the intercentre linkages which define the areal extent of a central place system. The technique developed below is based upon the use of interviews, but it differs in two important respects from the approach of the studies just cited. First, it takes the central place as the basic unit of analysis, rather than the individual type of business, the individual merchant, or the consumer. Secondly, it does not seek primarily to delimit the umland of a town, but rather to specify the types of shopping linkage which exist throughout a regional network of central places.

It is axiomatic that the existence of a central place system depends upon specific shopping connections between centres. If these connections are themselves suitably categorized, it becomes possible to define a system in terms of the presence of certain types of interaction among the member centres. With this approach, as will be seen, the delimitation of a centre's umland is a by-product of the identification of its central place system, rather than vice versa.

---

[6]Robert E. Dickinson, "The Regional Functions and Zones of Influence of Leeds and Bradford, " Geography, Vol. 15 (1929-30), 548-557; R. Cassady and H. J. Ostlund, The Retail Distribution Structure of the Small City, University of Minnesota Studies in Economics and Business No. 12 (Minneapolis: University of Minnesota, 1935); G. F. Deasy, "Sales and Service Industries in Luce County, Michigan, " Economic Geography, Vol. 26 (1950), 315-324; A Retail Trading Area Analysis of Jefferson, Iowa (Iowa City: Bureau of Business and Economic Research, University of Iowa, 1965).

Classification of Centres
by Spatial Interaction

Let CC denote the central city which is the focus of the system the investigator wishes to study. Depending on its relationship to CC, every other central place on earth may be placed in one, and only one, of the six categories below. These categories are based upon field experience, and they are not as complex in application as they perhaps appear in the abstract. The full classification is set out first, with commentary following.

1. Non-competitive centre, NC:
   (a) its residents do not patronize functions performed in CC;
   (b) its residents do not patronize functions performed in any centre whose residents do patronize functions performed in CC;
   (c) its functions are not patronized by residents of CC or by residents of any centre whose residents do patronize functions in CC.

2. Major competitive centre, MC:
   (a) its residents do not patronize functions in CC;
   (b) its residents do not patronize functions in any centre whose residents do patronize functions in CC;
   (c) its functions are patronized by residents of CC or by residents of one or more centres whose residents do patronize functions performed in CC.

3. Primary tributary centre, PT:
   (a) its residents do patronize functions in CC;
   (b) its residents either do not patronize functions in any MC centre, or their reliance on such a centre is less than their reliance on CC;
   (c) its residents may or may not patronize functions in centres other than CC and one or more MC centres, but this fact is not relevant for the classification.

4. Secondary tributary centre, ST:
   (a) its residents do patronize functions in CC;
   (b) its residents do patronize functions in one or more MC centres, and their reliance on at least one such centre is more than their reliance on CC;
   (c) its residents may or may not patronize functions in centres other than CC and one or more MC centres, but this fact is not relevant for the classification.

72

5. Primary peripheral centre, PP:

   (a) its residents do not patronize functions in CC;

   (b) its residents do patronize functions in one or more centres whose residents do patronize functions in CC;

   (c) its residents rely on a PT centre more than on any other type of centre.

6. Secondary peripheral centre, SP:

   (a) its residents do not patronize functions in CC;

   (b) its residents do patronize functions in one or more centres whose residents do patronize functions in CC;

   (c) its residents rely on either an ST centre or an MC centre more than on any other type of centre.

The first point to be made with respect to this classification is that the central city, CC, may be any central place whatsoever. If CC is a small centre, it is likely that the last two categories described above, or even the last four, will not be represented; but all six categories will normally be present when CC is a medium-sized or large central place. It is important to note that the category to which a given central place belongs can change as CC is changed. It must always be remembered that the entire classification is based upon a specific, designated centre whose central place system is the focus of interest. Assuming that one goal of geographic research is the establishment of general statements of wide applicability, this systems concept will in practice normally be applied to large rather than small central cities. However, there is nothing in the logic of the classification which precludes its application to even the smallest hamlet.

Once CC has been selected, the next task is to classify all other central places. This can only be accomplished by fieldwork, since comprehensive documentary records of intercentre linkages are not available. In carrying out the fieldwork, however, it is not necessary to make a detailed investigation of consumer movements in terms of trip frequencies and expenditures for individual goods. What matters, from the point of view of the urban system as a whole, is simply whether or not one centre normally relies on another for some goods and services. In other words, the unit of analysis at the system level is the central place, not the central function or the individual consumer. The functional complexity of central places presumably rests on a myriad of individual consumer behaviour patterns, but it is the former, not the latter, which is the primary focus of interest in the present context.

Typically, a central place relies upon one or more other centres for certain functions, and in turn is relied upon for other functions by lesser centres. Therefore, for each centre, field interviews are designed to identify (a) the centres upon which the centre in question relies, and (b) the centres which rely upon the centre in question. It will be seen that (a) and (b), when established for a large number of centres over a wide area, form two sets of information which can be used as a check on each other. This information then becomes the basis for classifying centres and delimiting a central place system.

Before looking more closely at the proposed classification of centres, a few additional words on field methodology are in order. Experience shows that the best informants are persons who are themselves involved in retail and service businesses. These persons not only tend to treat the interviewer with less suspicion than do housewives; they are also in a position to comment on <u>both</u> (a) <u>and</u> (b) above, rather than on (a) alone. Where available, bank managers, newspaper publishers, and officials of Chambers of Commerce are in general particularly knowledgeable and helpful.

The interviews themselves are most productive when no formal schedule of questions is used. The informal style of interview, moreover, is facilitated by the fact that the analysis does not require highly detailed information at this stage. The interviewer wishes only to learn about linkages involving the centre in which the interview is taking place, and a great deal of relevant information can usually be elicited simply by asking where people go on out-of-town shopping trips, and where they come from to shop in the centre being analyzed. The answers can be verified and illuminated by inquiring why people do <u>not</u> patronize particular alternative centres. Other interviews, including those in other centres, provide further corroboration.

Virtually all intercentre linkages are identified consistently and unambiguously by all informants. In a very few cases, however, some probing and perhaps more interviews than usual are necessary to establish which of two or more centres a given centre relies on most strongly. In all cases examined during this study, there has been no doubt regarding how each centre should be categorized with respect to the central city whose system is under investigation.

The six categories in the proposed classification are illustrated in Figure 11. Referring to the description of each category given above, it can be seen that non-competitive centres (NC in Figure 11), and major competitive centres (MC), are identical in all respects but one. They are alike in that they themselves patronize neither the central city (CC), nor any centre which itself patronizes the central city. They differ in that major competitive centres are patronized either by the central city or by centres which patronize the central city, while non-competitive centres are not thus patronized.

The functional development of any central place is affected by the commercial status of the centre or centres to which it is tributary. Hence, major competitive centres can affect the growth of centres tributary to the central city; while non-competitive centres cannot. More specifically, a major competitive centre may, through either a restrictive or a permissive influence on a centre tributary to the central city, distort hierarchical regularities in the central city's central place system. A non-competitive centre, by definition, can have no such influence. The difference between non-competitive centres and major competitive centres is thus critical, since it separates centres which may have an effect on the central city's system from those which cannot do so.

In an empirical study, the category of non-competitive centres accounts for most of the central places on earth. The category of major competitive centres, on the other hand, is composed of only a few places; but these places are extremely important because, as will be shown, they set limits to the extent of the central city's system. The term "major competitive centre" is not entirely satisfactory, but it is consistent with the fact that any centre within the central city's system (which major competitive centres are not), is a "minor" competitive centre of the central city with regard to certain functions. More important than their name, however, is the fact that the major competitive centres of any given central city are by no means similar to one another in size and functional complexity. Some are small but relatively close to the central city, whereas others are large but far away. To take an example from the empirical material presented later, the major competitive cen-

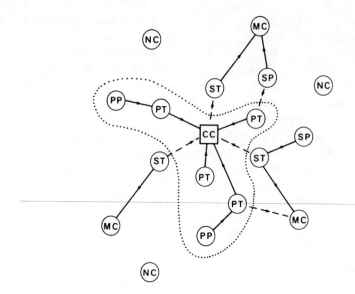

CC	Central City	MC	Major Competitive Centre
PT	Primary Tributary Centre	NC	Non-Competitive Centre
PP	Primary Peripheral Centre	──▶	Main Allegiance
ST	Secondary Tributary Centre	─▶─	Minor Allegiance
SP	Secondary Peripheral Centre	·······	Limit of CC 's System

Figure 11. A System of Central Places

tres of Owen Sound, Ontario (population 17, 421 in 1961), include towns as different as Kincardine (population 2, 841), and London (population 181, 283). Major competitive centres are alike only in their relationship to the central city which is the focus of the system under investigation.

The next two categories are those of primary tributary cen-tres (<u>PT</u>), and secondary tributary centres (<u>ST</u>). These two categories are alike in that primary and secondary tributary

76

centres both patronize the central city. The difference lies in the strength of their allegiance to the central city as compared with their allegiance to one or other of the central city's major competitive centres. A primary tributary centre places its main reliance on the central city, while a secondary tributary centre relies less on the central city than on a major competitive centre. Figure 11 illustrates these relationships.

Residents of a primary or secondary tributary centre may patronize functions in centres other than the central city and one or more major competitive centres. It is possible, though unlikely in reality, for a primary or secondary tributary centre to place greater reliance on another primary or secondary tributary centre than on either the central city or one of the latter's major competitive centres. However, from the point of view of the classification, the important question concerns only the relative pulls of the central city and the major competitive centre or centres. Suppose X is a centre whose residents patronize solely the central city. Clearly X is a primary tributary centre. Now suppose Y is a centre which relies primarily upon X, then upon one of the central city's major competitive centres, and only to a slight degree upon the central city itself. Despite its great reliance upon X, centre Y is classed as a secondary tributary centre, since it relies less on the central city than on the major competitive centre.

The final two categories have been designated primary peripheral centres (PP), and secondary peripheral centres (SP). These centres resemble those in the first two categories in that they do not patronize the central city. However, unlike major competitive centres and non-competitive centres, primary and secondary peripheral centres do patronize centres which themselves patronize the central city. A primary peripheral centre places its main reliance on a primary tributary centre of the central city. A secondary peripheral centre places its main reliance either on a secondary tributary centre of the central city, or on one of the latter's major competitive centres (see Figure 11).

In practice, primary and secondary peripheral centres are found to be few in number compared to primary and secondary tributary centres. They are normally small villages and hamlets in outlying districts from which the central city is relatively inaccessible. Moreover, the residents of these peripheral centres, at least in Ontario, are primarily retired farm couples whose needs are very simple, and whose fear of even moderately large towns is considerable. There are peripheral hamlets whose residents will not risk driving on paved roads, even to visit a nearby village; they prefer the relative calm of the gravel-surfaced side roads, and they visit the larger towns as infrequently as possible. It is evident that the failure of peripheral centres to patronize the central city is not merely a matter of physical inaccessibility.

Definition of a System

Given the above classification, the central place system of a particular town is defined to include the town itself together with all its primary tributary centres and all its primary peripheral centres (see Figure 11).

The rationale for this definition follows logically from the classification of centres. The system must contain those centres whose functional complexity is affected more by the central city than by any of the latter's major competitive centres. Moreover, the system must contain all centres to which this criterion applies. Non-competitive and major competitive centres are thus excluded, since the central city does not affect them at all. Secondary tributary centres, though influenced by the central city, are influenced even more by major competitive centres, and are also excluded. Primary tributary centres, on the other hand, are affected chiefly by the central city, and must be included in the system. In reality, most primary tributary centres are not at all affected by any of the central city's major competitive centres.

Primary peripheral centres are included in the system on the grounds that the central city influences their functional development indirectly through its influence on the functional development of primary tributary centres. Certainly, it can be argued that the development of a primary peripheral centre is more likely to be affected by the central city than by any of the latter's major competitive centres. Precisely the opposite is true in the case of secondary peripheral centres, and these are therefore excluded from the system, as shown in Figure 11.

In this fashion, the central place system of any centre, large or small, may be isolated for further study. The boundary of the system serves to delimit the umland of the central

city, and this approach thus makes it possible to delimit umlands in a manner which is not subject to the arbitrary selection
of a set of mutually competitive centres. It should be noted, in
this connection, that the umland boundary shown in Figure 11 is
derived from the identification of the central city's central place
system, rather than vice versa.

This method of identifying a central place system proceeds
without any need to investigate the shopping behaviour of the
dispersed population living outside the central places themselves. The question thus arises as to whether the present approach could be applied to the business districts within a
metropolitan area, where central places are commercial nodes
embedded in a continuous and densely populated matrix of consumers. In such an area, the necessary information on intercentre linkages would probably have to be obtained by interviewing
consumers in the act of shopping, in order to determine which
other centres they patronize. In principle, however, the proposed classification could still be applied.

The systems approach described, if consistently applied,
could bring to central place studies a welcome note of comparability which has hitherto largely been absent, and without which
the formulation of significant generalizations will remain difficult. The lack of any concept of a central place system has
been to date one of the major stumbling-blocks in empirical
work. No study can proceed without first delimiting a "study
area," yet the question of spatial specification thus presented
has previously not been fully recognized as a problem of fundamental importance. Study areas have been delimited arbitrarily, or at best in terms of political units, but never in terms
of relationships among the objects to be studied. The significance of the concept of a system of central places is obvious
once stated, but it has eluded researchers up to this point.

In analyzing central places to determine whether they are
hierarchically structured, the identification of a central place
system is only the first step. It is a vital step, because it ensures that subsequent stages of the analysis deal with an array
of centres known to form a meaningful functional whole. But
only two criteria of hierarchical structuring are thus applied:
that of the spatial interdependence of centres and that of completeness of the system. The third and fourth criteria, those
of discrete stratification of centrality and interstitial placement
of orders, are treated in the following section.

THE STRATIFICATION PROBLEM

Failure to address the stratification problem, like failure to identify meaningful systems of central places, is a major inadequacy of previous central place research. Theoretical considerations have revealed that the central places in an ideal hierarchy form groups at different levels of functional complexity. The mutual discreteness of these groups is perhaps the most distinctive feature of the ideal system, and is expressed in the criterion of discrete stratification of centrality. The practical application of this criterion calls first of all for an examination of methods of measuring urban centrality, and secondly for the establishment of a satisfactory technique for grouping the centrality values thus obtained.

Measuring Functional Complexity

An index of centrality must quantify in some reasonable way the extent to which a town provides surrounding consumers with goods and services. Among the attributes of a central place, three potential indices of centrality readily suggest themselves: the population of the centre; its number of central functions (that is, distinct types of retail and service business); and its number of central establishments (that is, separate retail and service firms regardless of type).

Population data are in general more easily obtainable than data on functions or establishments. However, it commonly occurs that part of the population of a place is engaged in pursuits other than serving extra-urban customers with consumer goods and services. That is to say, the economic base of a centre may involve more than just the performance of central place activities.[7] Thus, the presence of manufacturing in a place, or of major administrative or resort facilities, may swell its population without appreciably affecting its role as a central place, and so make it appear to possess greater centrality than is actually the case. Population size can nevertheless be a useful index of centrality in areas which are relatively devoid of manufacturing and other non-central-place activities, and for this reason such areas are preferred as central place

---

[7]Central place activities are clearly distinguished from other aspects of the economic bases of towns in Chauncy D. Harris and Edward L. Ullman, "The Nature of Cities," Annals of the American Academy of Political and Social Science, Vol. 242 (1945), 7-17.

"laboratories." However, population alone is generally an inadequate measure of a place's centrality.

A count of central functions or of central establishments would seem to provide a more direct measure of the attractiveness of towns to outside customers. However, it is not easy to decide which of these two variables is the more accurate index when taken singly. In support of using functions, it may be argued that towns attract trade in proportion to the number of different goods they offer. On the other hand, in defence of using establishments, it may be urged that trade is attracted in proportion to the amount of choice offered to the shopper with respect to individual goods. An intuitive hypothesis is that differences in numbers of functions become decreasingly important as one moves from small to large towns, while the significance of differences in numbers of establishments increases. However, there is as yet no empirical evidence on which to judge this hypothesis, and the most reasonable view is that the centrality of places is significantly affected by variations in the numbers of both establishments and functions. The desired index should therefore take account of differences in both variables.

In pursuing this line of thought, it must be remembered that a real central establishment, or function, normally supplies consumers with a sizeable inventory of different items, and rarely with a single good or service. Moreover, one particular good may well be supplied by several different functions—for example, insecticide by general stores, hardware stores, garden centres and department stores. These facts make it clear that a centrality index based on counts of functions and/or establishments necessarily involves collectivization of the elemental goods sold to consumers. In other words, the researcher is faced with a form of the "aggregation problem" common to many types of economic analysis. [8]

The aggregation of goods into establishments and functions, however, need not be cause for alarm. First, the progress of history has produced in the western world, if not also elsewhere,

---

[8] See Otis D. Duncan and others, Metropolis and Region (Baltimore: Johns Hopkins Press 1960), p. 51. Attention is also drawn to the presence of the aggregation problem in central place research by Wayne K. D. Davies, "Some Considerations of Scale in Central Place Analysis," Tijdschrift voor Economische en Sociale Geografie, Vol. 56 (1965), 221-227.

a rather standardized set of central functions. Hence, two places containing the same functions are likely to offer almost identical overall inventories of goods, and in this sense they will have the same centrality. Similarly, with regard to the duplication of establishments, three hardware stores are more likely to be equalled in attractiveness by three others than by two or four. Thus, an index based on the numbers of both functions and establishments in towns appears capable, in principle, of adequately representing their relative centrality. Finally, as shown earlier, it is possible to substitute the realistic concept of the multiple-good firm for the traditional device of the single-good firm without destroying the hierarchical structure of theoretical central place models. Therefore, quite apart from considerations of time and expense, analysis at the level of the individual good is unnecessary.

In connection with the fact that a particular good may be supplied by several different functions, it should be noted that, as towns increase in size and functional complexity, specialization takes place in business enterprises. [9] Thus garden centres, which cater to a narrower range of demands than hardware stores (and are also less ubiquitous), are more specialized than the latter; and hardware stores in turn are more specialized than general stores, even though all three may sell insecticide. The emergence of progressively more specialized firms is clearly a factor in the relative centrality of towns. However, the degree of such specialization is expressed in the appearance of distinct new types of enterprise, and is thus automatically incorporated in any index which takes account of all identifiably different functions.

It is important to recall that the concept of centrality refers to the attractiveness of a town from the point of view of consumers who live outside the town. It may therefore be suggested that even the use of functions and establishments, rather than population, has its drawbacks when a true picture of a town's centrality is desired. Non-central-place population may be present as a result of the town's performing a non-central-place activity such as manufacturing, and this "excess" population may be large enough to support establishments which could

[9]Otis D. Duncan, "Urbanization and Retail Specialization," Social Forces, Vol. 30 (1952), 267-271.

not otherwise survive. Indeed, regardless of the presence of non-central-place activities, Duncan has suggested that certain types of business appear simply because of the size of the intra-urban market, and not from any demand on the part of external consumers.[10] Moreover, even in a "pure" central place, it is clear that some portion of the available goods must be consumed within the centre itself. How can demand generated within a town be separated from demand generated outside?

This difficulty is less serious than it appears at first sight. Consider a small town which contains, among other establishments, one jewelry store. While some part of this establishment is admittedly supported by the residents of the town, any and all of its wares may be purchased by outside consumers. Hence, the whole store may be counted as contributing to the centrality of the town, even though the store might go out of business if the patronage of the town's own residents were somehow to be withdrawn. The same argument can be extended to all establishments in all centres. Thus, in using functions and establishments to assess the centrality of towns, the researcher can overlook the academically valid distinction between internally and externally generated demands.

A variation on this theme is provided by the case of an establishment which arises to serve internal demand and which is located outside the town's central business district. On the grounds that external consumers visit only the central business district when they come to town, such an isolated outlying establishment should be disregarded in assessing the town's centrality. This amounts to saying that the centrality of a central place depends only on the functions and establishments in its central business district. For small towns, this is a valid generalization, but there is no doubt that outside consumers are attracted in force to the principal outlying shopping facilities of larger centres. These facilities may take the form either of planned plazas or of natural ribbons of commercial development along the main roads leading from the town. Whenever they occur, they must be included in assessments of the centrality of towns.

[10]Otis D. Duncan, "Service Industries and the Urban Hierarchy," Regional Science Association, Papers and Proceedings, Vol. 5 (1959), 105-120; see also pp. 133-135 for a discussion of this paper by Berry.

Fleming has suggested that externally and internally generated demands for a town's central place activities can be separated through the analysis of census data on retail sales
volumes.[11] The procedure is to multiply the population of the
town by a national or regional figure for retail sales per capita
per annum, and then to subtract the result from the actual yearly
retail sales of the town as recorded in the census. The remaining "excess" retail sales are claimed to represent the centrality of the town.

This claim, however, is unjustified, for the method implicitly assumes that each town's population allocates to its home
town an identical proportion of its total retail expenditures.
Clearly, this assumption is very unrealistic. The proportion
of total retail expenditures which a town's people actually allo-
cate to their home town is not fixed, but increases with the size
and functional complexity of the home town. The apparent excess retail sales obtained by Fleming are thus not comparable
from town to town, nor is there any evident way in which they
could be appropriately adjusted. The procedure is therefore of
no value in the present context.

In the case of villages and hamlets, the amount of money
spent "out of town" by the centre's own residents may not even
be fully equalled by the money spent in the centre by consumers
from outside. Such a centre would have a "negative excess" of
retail sales. The fact that Fleming found no such case serves
to point up the non-availability of census data on retail sales
for towns below a certain size. For large towns, there is no
reason why data of this type cannot be used, without manipula-
tion, to corroborate in a general way an index of centrality
based on functions and establishments. However, any further
use of such data seems to be inappropriate.[12]

These considerations lead to acceptance of the central functions and establishments in places as the basic data for an adequate index of centrality. As the first step in constructing the

[11]J. B. Fleming, "An Analysis of Shops and Service Trades in Scottish Towns," Scottish
Geographical Magazine, Vol. 70 (1954), 97-106.

[12]For Canada, additional corroborative data are available in the form of records of the
annual revenue of every post office in the country. Though dealing with only one particular
function, these data have the advantage of being available for all centres, down to the level
of tiny hamlets with postal revenues under $100.00 per annum; see Canada, Postmaster
General, List of Post Offices with Revenues for the Year Ended March 31, 1961 (Ottawa:
Queen's Printer, 1961).

index, a complete inventory must be made of the number of establishments of each function present in every central business district in the central place system under investigation. If major outlying shopping districts which attract external consumers are present in any centre, their establishments too must be tallied. The inventory must be exhaustive rather than selective, because only an exhaustive inventory can pick out the finer differences between centres, and because every single establishment in the system contributes towards the centrality of places. Many of the necessary data can be obtained from published sources such as Dun and Bradstreet business directories, but it is always advisable to check these sources in the field.[13]

A Quantitative Index of Centrality

Based on such an inventory, the index of centrality employed in this study is taken directly from a recent paper by Davies.[14] For each function, the amount of centrality contributed to a place is taken to be proportional to the number of establishments of that function present in the place, with the total number of establishments of that function in the entire system having a combined centrality value of 100. Thus, if a particular function is represented throughout the whole system by 20 establishments, each of the latter contributes a score of 5 towards the centrality of the places in which they occur. If one place happens to have three establishments of this function, it scores 15 accordingly. Davies terms the centrality value of a single establishment of any function the location coefficient of that function, and defines it as follows:

$$C = 100 . t/T$$

where: C is the location coefficient of function t;
t is unity, representing one establishment of function t;
and T is the total number of establishments of function t in the system.

Once the location coefficient of every function has been calculated in this way, the numbers of establishments of each function in each place are multiplied by the appropriate location

---

[13]The published sources used as aids in this study are noted in chap. v below.

[14]Wayne K. D. Davies, "Centrality and the Central Place Hierarchy," Urban Studies, Vol. 4 (1967), 61-79.

coefficients to obtain the amounts of centrality conferred on each place by each function. Addition of these amounts then gives the final index of centrality for each centre, termed by Davies the centre's <u>functional index</u>.

The calculation of functional indices for a system of central places may be illustrated with reference to the hypothetical system represented in Tables 1 and 2. Table 1 gives the basic data. Ten central places, identified by the letters <u>A</u> through <u>J</u>, contain a total of 59 establishments of ten different functions. For legibility, the places in the table are ranked by the number of different functions they contain, and the functions are ranked by the number of different centres in which they occur. Notice that function number six is absent from centre <u>D</u> but present in centre <u>E</u>. In the real world, the presence of a particular function in one centre guarantees neither its presence in all centres with more functions, nor its absence from all centres with fewer functions. This type of "leakage" appears to be always present in real systems, but it is normally of minor proportions, as suggested by these hypothetical data.[15]

In order to obtain the location coefficients of the various functions, the establishment totals in Table 1 are entered <u>seriatim</u> in the formula given above. The location coefficients in turn are multiplied by the appropriate numbers of establishments to determine the amounts of centrality contributed by each function to each place. These amounts are shown in Table 2. Each column in this table sums to 100, which is by definition the total amount of centrality contributed to the system as a whole by each function. Summing horizontally gives the functional indices of the ten centres, and these indices appear at the right of Table 2. The total amount of centrality in the entire system, since there are ten different functions, is 1,000, and the functional indices of the centres must of course sum to this amount.

---

[15]In the terminology of the Guttman scaling technique of social psychologists, to which the present form of tabulation bears a generic resemblance, function number six in Table 1 is the only function which is not a "perfect scale type." See Edward Hassinger, "The Relationship of Retail-Service Patterns to Trade-Center Population Change," <u>Rural Sociology</u>, Vol. 22 (1957), 235-240; Glenn V. Fuguitt and Nora A. Deeley, "Retail Service Patterns and Small Town Population Change: A Replication of Hassinger's Study," <u>Rural Sociology</u>, Vol. 31 (1966), 53-63.

TABLE 1. CENTRAL FUNCTIONS IN A
HYPOTHETICAL CENTRAL PLACE SYSTEM

Places	Functions										Total Establishments
	1	2	3	4	5	6	7	8	9	10	
A	4	2	3	1	2	1	2	1	1	1	18
B	3	1	3	1	1	1					10
C	2	1	1	1	1	1					7
D	3	1	2	1	1						8
E	2	1	1	1		1					6
F	2	1									3
G	1	1									2
H	1	1									2
I	1	1									2
J	1										1
Establish-ments	20	10	10	5	5	4	2	1	1	1	59
Location Coefficient	5	10	10	20	20	25	50	100	100	100	

TABLE 2. CENTRALITY IN THE SYSTEM SHOWN IN TABLE 1

Places	Functions										Functional Index
	1	2	3	4	5	6	7	8	9	10	
A	20	20	30	20	40	25	100	100	100	100	555
B	15	10	30	20	20	25					120
C	10	10	10	20	20	25					95
D	15	10	20	20	20						85
E	10	10	10	20		25					75
F	10	10									20
G	5	10									15
H	5	10									15
I	5	10									15
J	5										5
Total Centrality	100	100	100	100	100	100	100	100	100	100	1,000

The functional indices thus derived take account of variations between centres both in numbers of functions and in numbers of establishments. The presence in a centre of one establishment of a rare function can add more to that centre's centrality than the presence of several establishments of a ubiquitous function, and this accords with everyday experience. Similarly, duplication of establishments of a rare function is worth more in centrality than duplication of establishments of a ubiquitous function. The net result of this technique is to show centrality differences between centres with greater realism than would be achieved by the use of either functions or establishments alone. Notice in the tables, for example, that centre $\underline{A}$ has twice as many functions and three times as many establishments as centre $\underline{E}$, but that its functional index is more than seven times as high.

It will be noted that the location coefficient of a function is conceptually similar to the well-known location quotient used as a measure of the concentration of industrial activity in economic geography.[16] In particular, like the location quotient, the location coefficient is properly applied only to an array of places which is believed to constitute in some sense a meaningful system of interrelated entities. Davies was aware of this limitation, and he simply assumed that his arbitrarily delimited study area in South Wales was in fact a complete system of centres.[17] It is clear, however, that the addition or subtraction of a few centres would automatically change the location coefficients of functions, and hence the functional indices of towns. To ensure consistency, it is submitted that the location coefficient technique should be applied only to an array of central places which has been shown to constitute a system in the manner described in the previous section of this chapter. In this way, comparability of results can be achieved in future replicative studies.

In calculating location coefficients, the total amount of centrality attributed to each function is set at 100 units, and it may seem questionable to regard these amounts as equal. This practice, however, is justified so long as the central places under investigation comprise a complete system. With respect to the

[16]For a description of the location quotient, see John W. Alexander, Economic Geography (Englewood Cliffs, New Jersey: Prentice-Hall, 1963), pp. 594-595.

[17]Davies, "Centrality and the Central Place Hierarchy," 61-62.

consumers in such a system, each function may be thought of as a self-contained sub-system within the network of places. If the system contains, for example, fifty hardware stores and only five florists, it is these totals which limit the shopping alternatives of consumers with regard to these functions. One's choice among hardware stores is in principle ten times as free as one's choice among florists, since one can only patronize establishments within the system of which one is a part. It therefore seems reasonable to regard as equal the total amounts of centrality contributed to the system as a whole by each function.

Davies indicates that the location coefficient technique can be modified by using the number of employees in each function instead of the number of establishments. With this change, the employee becomes the basic unit of centrality in place of the establishment. Hence, the fact that establishments of certain functions vary in size is taken into account. However, a serious difficulty is presented by the general lack of published data on employment for small centres. Using employment data for one small area collected in the field, Davies compared functional indices based on these data with those based on numbers of establishments. The comparison revealed a tendency for the functional indices of the largest centres to be relatively larger when employees were used instead of establishments; and this was taken to reflect the fact that, for several functions, establishment size as measured by number of employees tends to increase with size of centre. However, when the centres were separately ranked by the two sets of functional indices, rank differences were found to be very minor. In general, differences between the two methods are not sufficient to justify the greatly increased effort which would be required to obtain the necessary employment data for extensive areas. [18]

Grouping Centrality Values

Theory states that all the centres in a given order of an ideal hierarchy are identical in functional complexity. This means that the centres in a given order would all have the same functional index, and the number of different functional indices in the system would be the same as the number of orders in the

[18] Ibid., 61-79.

hierarchy. Hence, in grouping the centres into orders, it could be said not only that the groups were mutually discrete, but also that within-group differences in centrality were zero.

While central place models are essentially static, centres in the real world evolve. Since potential entrepreneurs in reality do not have the perfect knowledge attributed to them in theory, the functional development of real centres should not be assumed to take place with the precision and simultaneity suggested by the models. In addition, real entrepreneurs may occasionally select economically sub-optimal locations for non-economic reasons, and the centrality of a place may be further affected by the presence of manufacturing or other non-central-place activities. Therefore, in grouping the members of a real central place system, the theoretical criterion that within-group differences in centrality are zero must be relaxed. It seems reasonable to substitute the rule that, for any two adjacent groups of centres, the between-group difference in centrality must be greater than, or at least equal to, the within-group differences. This rule has been termed the criterion of discrete stratification of centrality. Previous researchers have in general failed to observe even this relaxed and flexible criterion of hierarchical structuring.

The criterion of discrete stratification of centrality is applied as follows. The functional indices of the centres in a properly identified central place system are regarded as values on a linear scale of centrality, and the centrality difference between any two centres is calculated by simple subtraction. The presence or absence of groups satisfying the above criterion is then determined by inspection.

As an illustration, consider the functional indices appearing at the right of Table 2. These indices can be divided into three groups for which between-group differences are larger than within-group differences, as follows:

Group 1: centre A; index value 555;
Group 2: centres B through E; index values 75 to 120;
Group 3: centres F through J; index values 5 to 20.

A system such as this, in which the criterion of discrete stratification of centrality is not violated, is termed a perfect hierarchical system.

A word of caution must be entered at this point, for there may be more than one way in which the array of functional index values can be validly grouped. Thus, the criterion is not violated if the indices in Table 2 are grouped as follows:

Group 1: centre A; index value 555;
Group 2: centre B; index value 120;
Group 3: centres C through E; index values 75 to 95;
Group 4: centres F through I; index values 15 to 20;
Group 5: centre J; index value 5.

When two or more arithmetically valid groupings occur, the appropriate choice is facilitated by referring back to the original data on functional complexity, as shown in Table 1. These data indicate, in this case, that it is rather far-fetched to regard centre B as constituting a separate functional order. The removal from centre B of one establishment of function number three, for example, would change the functional indices of centres A through E enough to necessitate grouping B with centres C through E. Similarly, hamlet J is hardly likely to be considered a distinct hierarchical order on its own.

Additional assistance in solving this problem is obtained by application of the fourth criterion of hierarchical structuring: that of the interstitial placement of orders. In general terms, this criterion states that the actual distribution of central places on the landscape must strongly resemble one or other of the hierarchical models discussed in chapter ii. It is necessary to consider what is implied by the words "strongly resemble" in this criterion.

Of all the criteria of hierarchical structuring, that of the interstitial placement of orders is by far the most difficult to translate into workable rules for use in empirical studies. At one extreme, one might require that a system of centres conforms precisely to some theoretical model—for example, that shown in Figure 7. Such a posture, however, is out of keeping with the view that rigid adherence to the precision of the models is inappropriate in evaluating real world systems. At the other extreme, one might merely require that the centres in each order occupy the interstices in the pattern formed by places of higher rank, but this injunction seems too vague to be of much help. Suppose it is clear that a particular system conforms, in its general aspects, to the Versorgungsprinzip model. Should this system be deemed non-hierarchical if one or two interstices in the "town" pattern lack "villages"? What if a few interstices contain two centres of "village" stature? How many deviant in-

91

terstices does it take to condemn the system? What degree of distortion of the triangular lattice pattern of centres, regarding both distances and directions, may be tolerated?

No entirely satisfactory answers to these questions have been devised, and on the whole it seems that the attempt to formulate general rules for the application of this particular criterion is likely to remain unrewarding. Short of professing what might be termed locational agnosticism, the best that can be done is to deal in the subjective. Given the complexities of the real world, the criterion of interstitial placement of orders should not be taken to imply geometric precision in the distribution of actual towns. Rather, one should look for an arrangement in which one or other of the theoretical models can readily be recognized, but in a form which is stretched and distorted, with extra centres in some interstices, and centres missing from others.

In the hypothetical case above, it may be assumed that the spatial arrangement of centres A through J conforms to, say, the Versorgungsprinzip model, and verifies the grouping of the functional indices into three orders rather than four or five. The application of the criterion of interstitial placement of orders to real systems of centres is illustrated in the following chapter.

An alternative approach to the problem of correctly choosing one out of two or more arithmetically valid groupings of centrality values might be to devise quantitative rules pertaining to the functional similarity or dissimilarity of pairs of centres. Experience shows, however, that the diversity of condition encountered in case studies makes universal rules of this type difficult to formulate. It is felt to be both safer and more practicable to rely on intelligent interpretation of the original data and of the criterion of interstitial placement of orders whenever this problem arises.

Perfect and Imperfect Hierarchies

Failing the existence of a perfect hierarchical system, it may yet be discovered that places do exhibit some tendency to cluster at certain levels of centrality. It may be that one or two groups of centres satisfy the criterion of discrete stratification, while others do not; or it may be that the criterion would be satisfied if a relatively small number of centres were to have different

92

centrality values. In such cases, it is likely that the "stragglers" are centres which contain disproportionate amounts of non-central-place activities, and of course this possibility is open to empirical investigation. Where distortions of this nature occur, it certainly seems reasonable to regard the system as nevertheless essentially hierarchical.

It is therefore proposed that the term imperfect hierarchical system be given to any central place system which, as it stands, does not satisfy the criterion of discrete stratification of centrality, but which could be made into a perfect hierarchical system by arbitrary adjustment of the functional indices of not more than twenty per cent of all centres.

Once again, the criterion of interstitial placement of orders must be brought in, this time to determine the direction in which the functional index of each straggler ought to be adjusted. Suppose a particular centre has a functional index which lies in the middle of an otherwise clear break between "towns" and "villages." It is relative location, evaluated through the application of the criterion of interstitial placement of orders, which alone provides a basis for deciding whether this centre should be regarded as an "under-endowed town" or an "over-endowed village." The distinction is important, since these two labels identify two quite different abnormalities in a system which otherwise conforms to a model pattern.

It should be apparent that the two criteria of discrete stratification of centrality and interstitial placement of orders must always be considered together when real central place systems are being analyzed. It is an inescapable conclusion from central place theory that relative functional complexity and relative location are inextricably intertwined; each inevitably implies the other. It is for this reason that these two criteria are dealt with together in this discussion of the stratification problem.

In effect, then, three classes of central place systems are here proposed. First, a system is perfectly hierarchical if its centres satisfy the criterion that, for any two adjacent groups of centres, the between-group difference in centrality is equal to, or greater than, the within-group differences. Secondly, a system is imperfectly hierarchical if it can be made to satisfy the above criterion by arbitrary adjustment of the centrality values of not more than twenty per cent of all centres. Thirdly, a system which satisfies neither of the above conditions is

93

classed as a <u>non-hierarchical</u> system.

The use of the Davies functional index as a measure of centrality, and the application of these criteria for perfect and imperfect hierarchical systems, represent attempts to standardize in a meaningful way the procedures of empirical research. The concept of a system of centres is itself another such attempt. This discussion of the stratification problem concludes a treatment of four of the seven basic criteria of hierarchical structuring, namely those of the spatial interdependence of centres, completeness of the spatial system, discrete stratification of centrality, and interstitial placement of orders.

OTHER ASPECTS OF
EMPIRICAL WORK

The Remaining Diagnostic Criteria

The first of the three remaining criteria of hierarchical structuring has been termed the criterion of incremental baskets of goods. This criterion formally states that each centre in a given order in a central place hierarchy performs virtually all the functions present in centres in lower orders, plus an additional number of functions not normally performed in lower orders. It is important to note that this phrasing does not require each centre to perform <u>all</u> the functions performed in centres having lower centrality. Were the criterion to insist upon the latter, it is likely that it could never be satisfied in the real world.

Experience shows that real central place systems "leak" in the sense that the presence of a function in one place does not guarantee either its presence in all places with greater centrality or its absence from all places with less centrality. A hypothetical example is provided by function number six in Table 1, which is absent from centre $\underline{D}$ but present in centre $\underline{E}$. This type of leakage in real systems occurs whether places are ranked by their functional indices, by their populations, or by their numbers of functions or establishments.

In theoretical models of the central place hierarchy, each centre performs literally all the functions present in centres of lower order. However, since functional leakage seems to be invariably present in reality, little is gained by formulating a

94

diagnostic standard which can only be met in the absence of such leakage. Hence, the criterion of incremental baskets of goods is relaxed to the form stated above, just as the criterion of discrete stratification of centrality was also relaxed.

Among all empirical studies in which the relevant data are recorded, there is no case in which the criterion of incremental baskets of goods is not satisfied.[19] An occasional function is indeed found to have a very irregular pattern of occurrence, as is true of the hay, grain, and feed dealer of the case study presented in the following chapters. Normally, however, functional leakage is not of major proportions, and the application of this criterion is in practice largely a formality. None the less, the criterion in itself is important, since it implies that lists of functions diagnostic of each order can be drawn up for hierarchical systems. An interesting field for comparative study is thus opened up, and will be touched upon again in due course.

The remaining two criteria of hierarchical structuring require, first, that there be a minimum of three orders in the system, and secondly, that there be successively fewer centres in successively higher orders. The view that there must be at least three orders is primarily a matter of aesthetics. There is technically no reason why a small system, composed of a village and its few dependent hamlets, should not fulfill all the other criteria for a hierarchy, and it has earlier been suggested that the term "one-step hierarchy" be applied to such simple systems. One-step hierarchies, though doubtless ubiquitous, represent too elementary a level of organization to be of much interest to the researcher. In practice, by choosing at least a medium-sized town as the central city, systems will be found either to have at least three orders, or else to be non-hierarchical.

---

[19]As chapter iii has demonstrated, this is not to say that these studies identify valid hierarchies. Data sufficient for the application of the incremental goods criterion are available in the following: Leslie J. King, "The Functional Role of Small Towns in Canterbury," Proceedings of the Third New Zealand Geography Conference (Palmerston North: New Zealand Geographical Society, 1961), pp. 139-149; John R. Borchert and Russell B. Adams, Trade Centers and Trade Areas of the Upper Midwest, Urban Report No. 3 (Minneapolis: Upper Midwest Research and Development Council, 1963); Mauri Palomäki, "The Functional Centers and Areas of South Bothnia, Finland," Fennia, Vol. 88, No. 1 (1964), 1-235; David Grove and Laszlo Huszar, The Towns of Ghana: The Role of Service Centres in Regional Planning (Accra: Ghana Universities Press, 1964).

The final criterion calls for successively fewer centres in successively higher orders. This criterion is based, like all the others, on the characteristics of the theoretical models of the urban hierarchy. In Christaller's models, the numbers of centres in successive orders are related by a constant multiplier, but it seems reasonable, in keeping with the principle of making empirical criteria flexible, to insist only upon a pyramidal sequence of numbers of centres in successive ranks. Such a view accords with the fact that large centres are less numerous than small ones. This criterion also, like the criterion of incremental baskets of goods, suggests the possibility of comparative studies, since different hierarchical systems may exhibit different numerical pyramids.

Distribution of Centrality by Orders

When a central place system is found to be hierarchical, it is of interest to examine the manner in which the total centrality in the system is distributed among the various orders. Consider again the hypothetical system represented in Tables 1 and 2. This system is composed of three orders, with the following functional indices:

> Order 1: one centre; functional index 555;
> Order 2: four centres; functional indices 120, 95, 85 and 75;
> Order 3: five centres; functional indices 20, 15, 15, 15
> and 5.

These data may be rewritten as follows:

> Order 1: one centre; total centrality 555;
> Order 2: four centres; total centrality 375;
> Order 3: five centres; total centrality 70.

The centrality value of each order may then be expressed as a percentage of the total centrality in the system, which in this case is 1,000:

> Order 1: 55.5 per cent of total centrality;
> Order 2: 37.5 per cent of total centrality;
> Order 3: 7.0 per cent of total centrality.

As long as the basic data on functions and establishments are directly comparable, the analysis of several hierarchical systems in this way would generate comparative statistics which would present a number of questions for further research. For example, what are the limits to the percentage of total centrality which can be concentrated in the central city? What factors

96

cause this percentage to vary from system to system? Do the percentages in real systems always decrease in successively lower orders, and if so, why?

This method of analysis can only be applied to central place systems which are hierarchically structured. Other methods are available, however, which can be used whether hierarchical structuring is present or not.

Analysis of Thresholds

The threshold of a function is defined as the minimum number of consumers necessary to support the performance of that function. Strictly speaking, the concept of threshold refers to purchasing power rather than numbers of people; however, data on purchasing power are rarely easy to obtain, and the areas occupied by most central place systems are of sufficient economic homogeneity to justify the use of population data as a substitute. A more significant feature of existing threshold studies is that they express the threshold of a function as the size of the smallest centre in which the function normally appears, even though the effective threshold includes dispersed external consumers as well as the residents of the central place itself.[20] This practice results partly from the difficulty of securing accurate estimates of the numbers of external consumers involved, and partly from the fact that size of centre is a more readily visualized variable than total supporting population. It must be borne in mind, however, that size of centre may not be a constant proportion of total effective threshold.

Attention was drawn above to the phenomenon of functional leakage in central place systems. Because of this phenomenon, it is not always easy to determine the threshold of a function. If the centres in a system are ranked by population, functions which do not suffer from leakage will be found to have definite thresholds, above which they are always present and below which they never occur. Functions with leakage, however, do not have clear-cut entry levels, and for them some arbitrary rule to establish a threshold is necessary.

One possible rule would be to regard the smallest centre possessing a given function as representing the threshold size

---

[20]See, for example, Brian J. L. Berry and William L. Garrison, "A Note on Central Place Theory and the Range of a Good," Economic Geography, Vol. 34 (1958), 304-311; King, "The Functional Role of Small Towns in Canterbury."

of centre for that function. There are cases, however, where a function which is usually confined to large and medium-sized towns crops up anomalously in one or two very small centres; an example is provided by hardware stores in the systems examined later in this study. In such cases, the smallest centre performing the function is by no means an accurate indicator of the function's normal entry level.

A more satisfactory rule is to define the threshold as that size of centre which divides the ranked list of centres in such a way that the number of centres lacking the function above the division is equal to the number of centres possessing the function below the division. An example will make this clear. Table 3 presents some hypothetical data regarding the occurrence of three particular functions in a ranked list of towns. For function X, the above rule gives a population of 600 as the threshold size of centre, since function X is absent once above centre number six, and present once below it. For function Y, the corresponding threshold value is 450 people, and for function Z, 650 people. Note that the patterns of occurrence of functions Y and Z make it necessary in each case to average the populations of two adjacent centres in order to obtain the required results. Note also that duplication of establishments, which occurs in certain centres, is disregarded while these calculations are being carried out.[21]

While the above rule identifies thresholds objectively, a few functions have such irregular patterns of occurrence that the whole concept of threshold seems quite meaningless when applied to them. This type of situation, which admittedly is not common, is illustrated by function Z in Table 3. Here, the objective application of the rule yields a threshold value of 650 people, yet it seems rather far-fetched to regard this function as having a valid threshold at all. In practice, this situation tends to arise in the case of certain kinds of agricultural supply

[21]This rule for determining thresholds was proposed in P. Haggett and K. A. Gunawardena, "Determination of Population Thresholds for Settlement Functions by the Reed-Muench Method," Professional Geographer, Vol. 16, No. 4 (July, 1964), 6-9; see also L. J. Reed and H. Muench, "A Simple Method of Estimating Fifty Per Cent Endpoints," American Journal of Hygiene, Vol. 27 (1938), 493-497. The paper by Haggett and Gunawardena contains a major misprint. The second sentence in the first paragraph on p. 8 should read as follows: "The curves for the two parameters cross at a population value at which the number of settlements without the function F$_j$ at this and greater sizes is equal to the number of settlements with that function at this and smaller sizes." The words in italics are reversed in the original.

TABLE 3. PATTERNS OF OCCURRENCE OF THREE FUNCTIONS
IN A HYPOTHETICAL CENTRAL PLACE SYSTEM

Rank of Centre	Population	Number of Establishments of		
		Function X	Function Y	Function Z
1	2,000	2	3	1
2	1,500	2	2	0
3	1,000	2	1	1
4	800	1	1	0
5	700	0	1	0
6	600	0	1	1
7	500	1	0	0
8	400	0	1	1
9	300	0	0	1
10	200	0	0	0

firms, such as implement and feed dealers. Though few in number, these firms can evidently operate in a small village as profitably as in a large town.

To eliminate functions of this type from further consideration, the following supplementary rule is proposed. Once a threshold has been determined as described above, this threshold (and the function to which it applies), will subsequently be disregarded unless at least half of all the centres above the threshold size possess the function in question. Applying this supplementary rule to the functions in Table 3, it is seen that function $\underline{Z}$ is eliminated from further consideration.

The determination of threshold values makes it possible to compare different central place systems with respect to the order of entry of functions. At present, only limited empirical data on thresholds are available, and these data have not been collected with reference to properly identified central place systems.[22] It is thus not known, for example, how variable the order of entry of functions in different systems can be, or what factors influence the variability of the thresholds of particular functions from region to region. Questions such as these

[22]See, for example, Brian J. L. Berry and William L. Garrison, "The Functional Bases of the Central Place Hierarchy," Economic Geography, Vol. 34 (1958), 145-154; King, "The Functional Role of Small Towns in Canterbury."

take on a special interest in the case of systems which are hierarchically structured, for it then becomes possible, as suggested above, to draw up lists of functions representing the incremental baskets of goods which are characteristic of each order. It has recently been suggested that individual functions may be incremental at successively higher orders in regions of progressively decreasing rural population density.[23] However, until the concept of a system of centres is applied in research, and until numerous studies using this concept are completed, this hypothesis cannot be fully verified.

Continuous Functional Relationships

A continuous functional relationship exists when there is a high statistical correlation between any two of the variables characteristic of the members of a system. The populations of centres, and the numbers of functions and establishments they contain, are three examples of such variables. An obvious fourth variable, but one devised too recently to have yet been incorporated in the search for correlations, is the centrality of centres as measured by the Davies functional index.

Evidence of continuous functional relationships was first published by Thomas. Using a sample of small towns in Iowa, Thomas showed that linear correlations existed between the populations of centres and their numbers of establishments, and also between their numbers of functions and the logarithms of their populations. The correlation coefficients for these relationships were 0.96 and 0.86 respectively.[24] The study by Thomas was later duplicated for small centres in Southern Illinois by Stafford, with similar results.[25] Additional data for other areas in the United States, with comparably high correlation coefficients, have been provided by Berry.[26]

The continuous functional relationships identified by these investigators are doubly provocative in view of the fact that the concept of a system of central places was not employed in any

[23]Brian J. L. Berry, Geography of Market Centers and Retail Distribution (Englewood Cliffs, New Jersey: Prentice-Hall, 1967), pp. 32-35.

[24]Edwin N. Thomas, "Some Comments on the Functional Bases for Small Iowa Towns," Iowa Business Digest, Vol. 31, No. 2 (February, 1960), 10-16.

[25]Howard A. Stafford, "The Functional Bases of Small Towns," Economic Geography, Vol. 39 (1963), 165-175.

[26]Berry, Geography of Market Centers and Retail Distribution, pp. 26-40.

of these studies. Even in the absence of this concept, important questions are stimulated by differences from region to region in the slopes of the regression lines, the values of the
correlation coefficients, and other features of these relationships. Were these differences to apply between properly identified systems of centres, their interpretation would be more
challenging still. Moreover, if continuous functional relationships were to be maintained whether or not the analysis dealt
with whole systems, there could well be grounds for hypotheses
of spatial organization transcending the level represented by
the existence of systems of centres. These considerations
should be kept in mind in future empirical studies.

The methods of analysis outlined above appear to be poten-
tially productive of useful generalizations concerning the nature
and interrelationships of central places. It bears repeating
that all of these techniques are founded upon an appreciation of
the concept of a system of centres. Some techniques, such as
the calculation of the percentages of centrality in successive
orders, are appropriate only for systems which are hierarchically structured. Others, notably the analysis of continuous
functional relationships, can be applied not only to all systems,
whether hierarchical or not, but also to arrays of centres
which do not constitute whole systems. Nevertheless, the concept of system is held to be basic to all analysis of central
place distributions. In the case study presented in the following
chapters, two central place systems are identified, and an attempt is made to suggest the value of the above techniques as
tools of comparative analysis.

MODELS AND EMPIRICAL RESEARCH

Since the criteria of hierarchical structuring employed in this
study are based upon theoretical models of the arrangement of
central places, it seems appropriate to comment on the relationship of models to empirical work. In particular, attention must
be given to the question of what constitutes an explanation of an
observed pattern of central places.

<u>Christaller's Empirical Procedure</u>

Christaller observed that central places in Bavaria were spaced on the average about five miles (seven to nine kilometres) apart, and he related this spacing to the length of a journey-hour during the time when the settlement pattern crystallized.[27] Then, believing that the overall distribution of Bavarian central places corresponded to the <u>Versorgungsprinzip</u> model, he calculated the distances which would separate adjacent centres of equal rank in this model when the distance between adjacent centres of the lowest rank was seven kilometres. Since the distance separating adjacent centres of any one rank in this model is $\sqrt{3}$ times the distance between adjacent centres of the next lower rank, the intercentre distances for successive ranks, beginning with the lowest, are 7, 12, 21, 36, 62, 108, and 187 kilometres.[28]

Christaller then selected a centre which he judged to be of the highest rank, such as München, Stuttgart, or Nürnberg-Fürth. On such a city, a <u>Versorgungsprinzip</u> model incorporating the above distances was mentally centred. Once oriented to accord with the locations of other centres judged to be of the highest rank, this model was used as a basis for "predicting" the locations of centres in all lower ranks. The locations of actual centres judged to be in each particular rank rarely coincided with the locations predicted by the model, and a large part of the empirical portion of Christaller's work consists of proposed explanations for either (a) the fact that a centre with the "right" amount of centrality deviates from the "right" location, or (b) the fact that a centre in the "right" location deviates from the "right" amount of centrality.[29]

[27] The journey-hour, or the distance that could comfortably be covered in one hour, is thought to have been the normal maximum distance travelled to market in the pre-industrial era, and thus to have been a basic determinant of the spacing of villages in Europe and Eastern North America. See Robert E. Dickinson, <u>City Region and Regionalism</u> (London: Routledge and Kegan Paul, 1947), pp. 29-30, 55; Lewis Keeble, <u>Principles and Practice of Town and Country Planning</u> (2nd edition; London: Estates Gazette, 1959), pp. 38-39. The basis of the constant <u>time</u> period in the phenomenon of the journey-hour apparently has not been explored.

[28] Walter Christaller, <u>Central Places in Southern Germany</u>, translated by Carlisle W. Baskin (Englewood Cliffs, New Jersey: Prentice-Hall, 1966), pp. 159-164.

[29] <u>Ibid.</u>, pp. 170-197. Baskin translates Christaller's <u>Versorgungsprinzip</u> analysis only for the case centred on München. A translation of the case centred on Stuttgart is available in H. Gardiner Barnum, <u>Market Centers and Hinterlands in Baden-Württemberg</u>, Department of Geography Research Paper No. 103 (Chicago: Department of Geography, University of Chicago, 1966), pp. 140-168.

The more recent model of Berry and Garrison, in which the Christallerian assumption of uniformly distributed purchasing power is abandoned, has made it clear that hierarchies can occur without the extreme geometric regularities of the earlier models.[30] However, the significance of Christaller's procedure does not lie in its use of a geometrically rigid model so much as in what it implies with respect to a methodology of explanation. The very act of proposing reasons for particular "deviations" from the "predictions" of the model involves the important assumption that the regularities of the model are inherent in reality, underlying whatever degree of chaos appears on the surface, and explaining reality insofar as the latter corresponds to the model. In other words, rationalizing deviations from the model can only be accepted as explanation if the model itself is accepted as "half" of the explanation of an observed pattern. The question that arises is whether there are any grounds for regarding a model as possessing explanatory power.

It is worth emphasizing that this question does not arise solely if the geometrically rigid models of Christaller are used. It also arises if spatial rigidity is abandoned in favour of Berry and Garrison's more flexible model, and if the criteria of hierarchical structuring developed in this study are applied. Suppose a case study finds a particular central place system to be an imperfect hierarchy. Are this system's "imperfections" to be accounted for as non-central-place deviations from an ideal system which is accepted as explaining the reality's underlying perfection? If not, how is the relative centrality of the places in the system to be explained? These questions transcend the particular form in which a model might be conceived.

Methodology of Explanation

In considering whether a model may be regarded as having explanatory power, three views appear to be logically defensible. The first may be elucidated by recalling that central place models are idealized representations of possible realities; they are imaginary, but they are not wholly a priori, since their premises are in essence simplifications of appropriate pieces of empirical knowledge. A central place model is therefore sim-

[30]Brian J. L. Berry and William L. Garrison, "Recent Developments of Central Place Theory," Regional Science Association, Papers and Proceedings, Vol. 4 (1958), 107-120.

ilar to the Weberian "ideal type" used in explanatory narratives by historians and sociologists. The use of ideal types as aids to explanation has been questioned by Watkins on the grounds that the same real situation can in principle result from entirely different sets of causes, so that correspondence between reality and an ideal type cannot guarantee that the latter contains the explanation of the former. On this view, even if a central place system corresponding perfectly to the Versorgungsprinzip model were discovered, the conclusion would have to be that no explanation of that system's characteristics could be guaranteed.[31]

The second view takes the doctrine of parsimony as its point of departure. If a model, however plausible, is inadmissible as explanation, how are the numbers, sizes, and spacing of central places to be explained? Presumably the only alternative would be to write a host of idiosyncratic histories of individual centres. This approach, however, would involve a great many more explanatory assumptions than would acceptance of a plausible model, and the doctrine of parsimony, as expressed in the maxim of Occam's Razor, therefore deems the latter to be the more defensible course. On this view, a full explanation has been given when deviations from the model have been satisfactorily rationalized.[32]

While a stand may be taken on either of the above positions, the third possible view recognizes that much of the difficulty stems from the equivocal nature of the terms "explanation" and "model." Explanations can themselves be grouped into several categories, and it is not easy to find a general answer to the question of what constitutes an explanation.[33] However, if Passmore's contention is accepted that explanation consists essentially in the removal or reduction of puzzlement, it certainly seems valid to regard a plausible model as an explanation, or partial explanation, of observed reality.[34]

[31]J. W. N. Watkins, "Ideal Types and Historical Explanation," British Journal for the Philosophy of Science, Vol. 3 (1952-53), 22-43.

[32]Entia praeter necessitatem non multiplicanda sunt. Loosely paraphrased, Occam's Razor states that the most plausible hypothesis is the one incorporating the fewest assumptions.

[33]From a geographer's viewpoint, despite the fact that geography is not mentioned in the discussion, the best extended analysis of types of explanation is Robert Brown, Explanation in Social Science (London: Routledge and Kegan Paul, 1963).

[34]John Passmore, "Explanation in Everyday Life, in Science, and in History," History and Theory, Vol. 2 (1962), 105-123.

The word "plausible" in the preceding sentence is important, for there is no doubt that models vary in their plausibility. Consider, for example, the case of the continuous functional relationships described in the previous section. The regression equation for the relationship between, say, populations and numbers of establishments would be described by many geographers as a "model" of the observed situation, but it is hard to see anything plausible in the statistical regularity expressed by the equation. The existence of the relationship, moreover, is not rendered noticeably less puzzling by the discovery of its mathematical expression. In other words, a model of no apparent plausibility is not capable of banishing puzzlement. It appears to follow that the degree of explanatory power possessed by a model increases with its plausibility.

The central place models of Christaller and Berry and Garrison, idealized though they are, depict eminently plausible landscapes. Each model's plausibility derives from the fact that the notions on which it is based accord well with intuitive conceptions of the way in which the real world operates. The concepts of threshold, range, and rational consumer behaviour are acceptable simplifications of what is honestly believed to exist. The central place model, unlike the regression model mentioned above, thus reduces puzzlement about reality by virtue of being deducible from premises which are themselves realistic. The semantic purist, it is true, might choose to hold that no part of reality is explained by the model per se, but that the concepts and interrelationships which fully explain the model also provide a partial explanation of reality. It is only a short step from this careful phrasing to the view that a central place model may be accepted as a partial explanation of observed distributions of towns.

The rationality of the concept of a hierarchy of market centres is further demonstrated by the fact that this concept has been consciously applied where opportunities have arisen for the planned creation of new patterns of settlement. The best known opportunities of this kind are undoubtedly those involving the construction of planned shopping centres in large cities, and here the concept of a hierarchy of neighbourhood, community, and regional centres is too familiar to require comment.[35] Of

[35]Most recently, see Walter D. Stoll, "Characteristics of Shopping Centers," Traffic Quarterly, Vol. 21 (1967), 159-177; on British practice, see Wilfred Burns, British Shopping Centres: New Trends in Layout and Distribution (London: L. Hill, 1959).

greater interest in the present context are cases where a pattern of market centres has been planned on the hierarchical principle for an open country area. Here, the development of new settlements on the polders is especially illuminating, since the Dutch appear to have initially used the hierarchy concept without knowledge of Christaller's work.[36] A second example of a planned open-country hierarchy is provided by the Israeli project on the Lakhish Plains running eastward from the Gaza Strip.[37] But the most interesting case of all is that of the aborted plans developed under the Third Reich for the "rationalization" of the pattern of market towns on the plains of Poland. These plans are known to have been based explicitly on Christaller's models, but the details are only slowly coming to light.[38]

These examples are practical illustrations of the plausibility of the concept of a hierarchy of central places. They support the contention that the hierarchy concept is realistic, and therefore possessed of explanatory power. The models of Christaller, and of Berry and Garrison, indeed go far towards resolving the puzzle presented by the actual distribution of central places. However, with these models accepted as partial explanations, there remains the question of how to account for observed deviations from perfect hierarchical structuring.

Departures from Hierarchical Structuring

In principle, departures from perfect hierarchical structuring can be grouped into two categories. First, there may be deviations resulting from the fact that central functions do not behave in quite as simple a manner as the models assume.

[36]Christaller is not mentioned in most of the works on this subject; see C. A. P. Takes, "The Settlement Pattern in the Dutch Zuiderzee Reclamation Scheme," Tijdschrift van het Koninklijk Nederlandsch Aardrijkskundig Genootschap, Vol. 77 (1960), 347-353; A. K. Constandse, "Reclamation and Colonisation of New Areas," Tijdschrift voor Economische en Sociale Geografie, Vol. 54 (1963), 41-45.

[37]Cited in Berry, Geography of Market Centers and Retail Distribution, p. 131.

[38]The plans are mentioned in a footnote in August Lösch, The Economics of Location, translated by William H. Woglom and Wolfgang F. Stolper (New Haven: Yale University Press, 1954), p. 132. Two recent articles in Polish develop the subject: Czeslawa Kaniowna, "Problem Osiedli Centralnych w Bylej Rejencji Opolskiej" ("The Problem of Central Settlements in the Old Province of Opole"), Materialy i Studia Opolskie, No. 4 (1963), 95-99; Stefan Golachowski, "Rola Teorii Christallera w Planowaniu Hitlerowskim na Slasku" ("The Role of Christaller's Theory in the Hitler Regime's Planning for the Province of Slask"), Studia Slaskie, No. 10 (1964), 167-177. For translations of these articles, I am indebted to Miss Joan Marchut.

Secondly, there may be deviations which result from the presence in towns of non-central-place activities.

The first type of deviation could occur if central functions departed widely from the assumed practice of appearing whenever their necessary threshold populations become available. Alternatively, the hierarchical structure could be destroyed if the thresholds and ranges of numerous individual functions were to vary radically from one part of a system to another. On the whole, it appears improbable that serious irregularities of this kind will occur, and the practical course is to assume that central functions behave consistently. It then follows that deviations from the models are to be rendered intelligible in terms of the presence of non-central-place activities, that is, manufacturing, mining, and other activities which do not directly serve the consumers in the immediate umland.

If the effects of non-central-place activities are to be considered, all occurrences of these activities in the system under investigation must be examined. It would be wrong to use the presence of non-central-place activities in explaining the centrality of centres which deviate from the model, while at the same time ignoring the presence of non-central-place activities in other centres which do not deviate. A complete knowledge of the non-central-place activities of any system is therefore as essential as an inventory of its central functions and establishments.

Since the hierarchical criterion of discrete stratification of centrality permits a degree of variability in the centrality of the centres in a particular order, there is room for subjectivity in the evaluation of the effects of non-central-place activities. Indeed, it could not be otherwise. The most that can be said, in the last analysis, is that the sizes and spacing of the towns forming a central place system have been satisfactorily explained when no glaring departures from the expected Christallerian pattern remain after non-central-place activities in all centres have been given due consideration.

Viewed thus as part of an explanatory methodology, a central place model amounts to more than just a taxonomic device. It is true that classification is a major objective of central place research, but the criteria enumerated in the present study are designed to ensure that the classes of centres which are identified are as far as possible inescapable, rather than arbitrary, in their composition. That is to say, valid orders of centres are real entities, and different investigators should not obtain different results in one and the same area. Hence, central place research is empowered to go beyond mere classification, and to engage in the hopefully serendipitous search for order in the size and spacing of towns. Insofar as the discovery of such order is a stated objective, geography is not, as Tatarkiewicz would have it, a typological rather than a nomological science.[39]

[39]Wladyslaw Tatarkiewicz, "Nomological and Typological Sciences," Journal of Philosophy, Vol. 57 (1960), 237.

V

The Barrie and Owen Sound
Systems: Locational Analysis

The case study reported in this and the following chapter provides concrete illustrations to accompany the preceding theoretical discussions. For convenience, the present chapter is
devoted primarily to a locational analysis of the selected central
place systems, while chapter vi deals with features which are
less explicitly spatial, such as thresholds of functions and continuous functional relationships.

GENERAL FEATURES
OF THE STUDY AREA

The selected area lies in the northern part of the peninsula of
Southern Ontario, as shown in Figure 12. The precise limits
of the study area are defined by the extent of the Barrie and
Owen Sound central place systems, but virtually all of the area
lies within the Counties of Simcoe, Grey, and Bruce. These
Counties were chosen principally because they form an agricultural zone in which manufacturing is relatively unimportant.
Figure 13 indicates that Simcoe, Grey, and Bruce Counties lie
north of the portion of Southern Ontario which can be regarded
as a Canadian extension of the American manufacturing belt.[1]

---

[1]Figure 13 may be compared with the maps of the American manufacturing belt in Gunnar
Alexandersson, Geography of Manufacturing (Englewood Cliffs, New Jersey: Prentice-Hall,
1967), pp. 40-41.

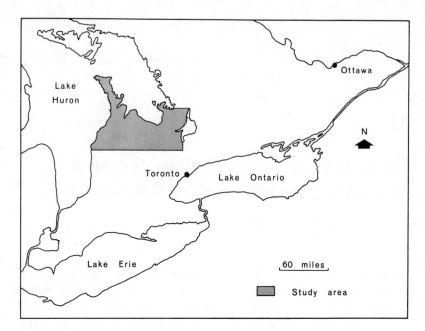

Figure 12. Location of Study Area

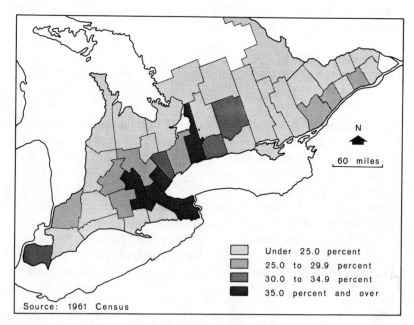

Source: 1961 Census

Figure 13. Employees in Manufacturing
(Per Cent of County Labour Force)

In a modern economy, manufacturing employs many more people than other non-central-place activities. In general, therefore, the probability that a central place system will exhibit perfect hierarchical structuring is inversely proportional to the amount of manufacturing activity the system contains. While other types of non-central-place activity, notably the tourist industry, occur in certain parts of the present study area, the relative absence of manufacturing makes the area a suitable one in which to test the concept of a hierarchy of central places. In short, most of the towns in the study area exist primarily as consumer service centres, and significant concentrations of non-central-place activities are few in number and readily identifiable.

The study area cannot be equated with the isotropic plain of classical central place theory, but its terrain is nevertheless far from rugged. Pleistocene ice covered all parts of Southern Ontario, and today the study area exhibits the undulating morainic surface which so often results from continental glaciation. In general, the only major relief features in the area are associated with the Niagara Escarpment, shown in Figure 14. The scarp face itself, rising as much as 800 feet above the adjacent lowland, is prominent along the Georgian Bay shore west of Collingwood. Behind Thornbury, the striking re-entrant of the Beaver Valley extends twenty miles southwards to a point near Flesherton. The Beaver Valley is one of four preglacial valleys in this section of the Niagara Escarpment, all of which now have the U-shaped cross-section associated with ice action. Behind Meaford is the Bighead Valley, broader and shallower than the Beaver Valley and not nearly as striking. The remaining two re-entrants, though of imposing proportions, are today flooded, and form Owen Sound and Colpoy Bay. The ports of Owen Sound and Wiarton thus have naturally protected harbours.[2]

With the exception of the Bruce Peninsula and some small, scattered tracts undergoing reforestation, all parts of the study area are farmed. In the Bruce Peninsula, the soils covering the dolomite caprock of the Niagara Escarpment are more than

[2]For detailed descriptions and excellent maps of surface features, see L. J. Chapman and D. F. Putnam, The Physiography of Southern Ontario (2nd edition; Toronto: University of Toronto Press, 1966), chaps. ii and iv. It should be noted that the paperback edition of this work lacks the portfolio of large-scale maps which accompanies the hardcover edition.

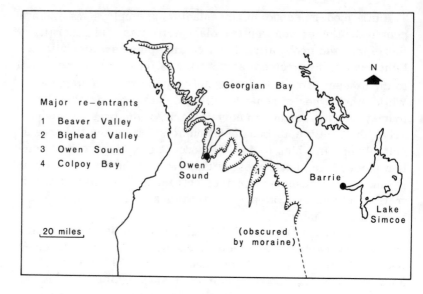

Figure 14. The Niagara Escarpment

usually shallow, and the area's remoteness from Southern
Ontario's main cities also militates against successful agriculture. The four Townships forming the peninsula remain today heavily wooded, with an overall population density of only
eight persons per square mile.[3]

Along a traverse from Lake Simcoe westwards to Lake
Huron, average farm size increases, while the density of the
farming population per square mile of land in farms declines.
In Simcoe County, average farm size in 1961 was 146 acres,
and there was a farming population density of 18 persons per
square mile. For Bruce County, the corres-
ponding figures were 180 acres and 14 persons.[4] In part, these
differences reflect the slightly lower fertility and the greater

[3]This figure includes the incorporated municipality of Lions Head, as well as unincorporated centres and dispersed population. Data on population are from the 1961 Census of
Canada, Vol. I, Part 1, Table 7. Areas of Townships are from the 1963 Municipal Directory, compiled by the Ontario Department of Municipal Affairs, Toronto. After 1963, the
latter publication ceased to provide data on the areas of municipalities.

[4]Ontario, Department of Economics and Development, Georgian Bay Region: Economic
Survey (Toronto: Ontario Department of Economics and Development, 1963), pp. 83, 100.

emphasis on livestock in the western part of the area. However, the figures are also affected by the presence of small, specialized fruit and vegetable farms in the east around Collingwood, Alliston, and Bradford.[5]

While the density of the farm population thus decreases steadily from east to west, the same is not true of the density of the farmers' purchasing power. In Simcoe County, the proportion of all commercial farms having gross sales valued at $5,000 or more in 1961 was 40 per cent. In Bruce County, the figure was 46 per cent; but in Grey County, lying <u>between</u> Simcoe and Bruce, the proportion was only 35 per cent.[6] These data suggest that, so far as the farming population is concerned, the density of purchasing power is lowest in the central part of the study area, and rises towards the eastern and western ends. This pattern should be borne in mind when the relative functional development of central places in different parts of the area is being evaluated.

The density of the total population outside incorporated centres, including nonfarm as well as farm households, varies generally between 10 and 40 persons per square mile. However, as shown in Figure 15, the density lies between 10 and 20 persons per square mile over the greater part of the study area, with higher values confined largely to Simcoe County. The five Townships with densities over 40 per square mile fall into two categories. First, there is Essa Township, southwest of Barrie, which contains Camp Borden with its complement of some 10,000 Canadian Armed Forces personnel. Secondly, there are high-density Townships adjacent to the four large towns of Barrie, Orillia, Midland, and Owen Sound, and field observations make it clear that overspill from these towns accounts for the increased densities in these localities. The fact that the distribution of rural population in the study area is not completely uniform should not be cause for concern, since Berry and Garrison have demonstrated that a central place

---

[5]Ibid., pp. 8-13; see also Willis B. Merriam, "Reclamation Economy in the Holland Marsh Area of Ontario," Journal of Geography, Vol. 60 (1961), 135-140.

[6]1961 Census of Canada, Vol. V, Part 2, Table 14. A farm is classified as "commercial" if it has gross sales valued at $1,200 or more per year. Generally speaking, a farmer is doing poorly if he is not grossing at least $5,000 per year from the sale of farm products.

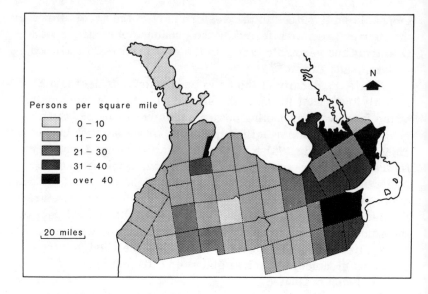

Figure 15.   Density of Unincorporated Population

hierarchy can exist in an area which is not absolutely isotropic. [7]
    A further relevant point is that the study area is completely
covered by a rectangular grid of improved roads spaced one
and a quarter to one and a half miles apart. These roads are
a legacy of the lot and concession land survey system of the
nineteenth century, a system similar in its essential aspects
to the township and range survey used in the interior of the
United States. The road net in the study area, as elsewhere in
Southern Ontario, contains minor departures from perfect rec-
tangularity, and here and there one encounters an unopened
road allowance; but these imperfections have a negligible effect on the movement of people and goods. In general, it can
be said that accessibility throughout the study area is simply
a function of distance.
    Four types of non-central-place activity are present in the
study area: manufacturing, wholesaling, the tourist industry,

[7]Brian J. L. Berry and William L. Garrison, "Recent Developments of Central Place
Theory, " Regional Science Association, Papers and Proceedings, Vol. 4 (1958), 107-120.

and the training of military personnel. None of these activities can be said to dominate the economy of the region as a whole, and all of them are highly localized, which facilitates an assessment of their probable effects upon the central place pattern. Manufacturing and wholesaling are overwhelmingly concentrated in Barrie, Owen Sound, and Collingwood, the three largest towns. The tourist industry affects all coastal or lakeside centres to some extent, but it is the dominant urbanizing force only at Wasaga Beach and Sauble Beach. Military training is localized at Camp Borden, mentioned above, which affects the centrality of the villages of Angus and Camp Borden, and also of Barrie, the nearest large town. Below, in the analysis of centrality, the effects of these non-central-place activities on the functional complexity of places is examined in detail.

In sum, the study area is endowed with the four features which make an area an adequate central place laboratory. The relief is generally low; there is a continuous veneer of rural population from which sharp discontinuities in density are absent; a dense road network provides ease of movement in all parts of the area; and there is a general absence of major concentrations of non-central-place activities. These attributes make the area an appropriate one in which to test the concept of hierarchical structuring.

THE CENTRAL PLACE
SYSTEMS: EXTENT AND SHAPE

Within the selected study area, the two incorporated cities of Barrie (21,169), and Owen Sound (17,421), stand out as the largest and most functionally complex central places.[8] These places were therefore designated central cities, and the areas covered by their respective central place systems were determined in the field in accordance with the technique described in the previous chapter. The results are shown in Figures 16 and 17.

Both Barrie and Owen Sound occupy distinctly eccentric locations within their systems. The eccentricity of Owen Sound

---

[8]Population figures following place names are taken from the 1961 Census of Canada.

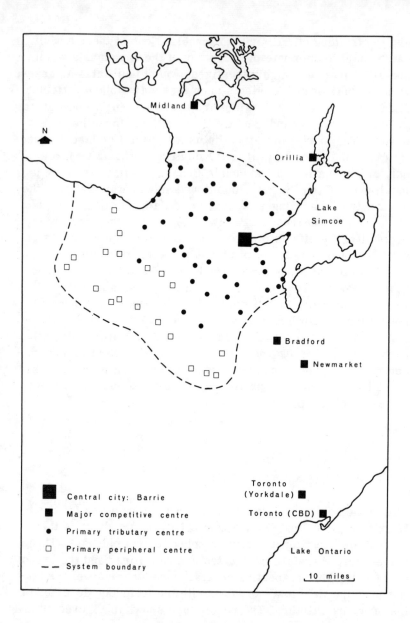

Figure 16. Barrie System: Centres Classed by Type

is even more apparent when it is recalled that the Bruce Peninsula supports a very sparse population; in fact, well over 80 per cent of the population in the Owen Sound system lives south

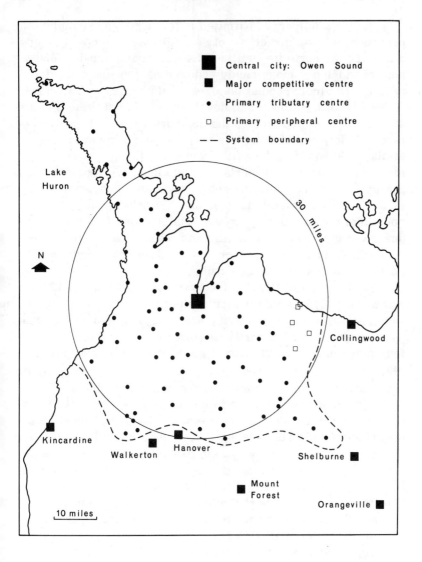

Figure 17. Owen Sound System: Centres Classed by Type

of the central city. In the case of Barrie, it is over 30 miles to the most distant parts of the system in the west, but a scant 10 miles brings one to the limits of Barrie's reach towards the north and the south.

Barrie's influence is limited in the north and south by the presence in those directions of several major competitive centres. To the north lie Orillia (15,345), and Midland (8,656), both of which are more richly endowed as consumer service centres than their population sizes would suggest. The relatively pronounced functional development of both these towns is a result of their location on the southern margin of the Muskoka lake district, one of Ontario's major summer resort areas. Midland, in addition, benefits from being the commercial focus for the cluster of small ports located elbow-to-elbow along this stretch of the Georgian Bay shore; together, Penetanguishene (5,340), Port McNicoll (1,053), and Victoria Harbour (1,066), contain almost as many people as Midland itself. As a consequence of the strength of Orillia and Midland as service centres, the Barrie central place system does not include the northern portion of Simcoe County.

To the south of Barrie, the towns of Bradford (2,342), and Newmarket (8,932), are major competitive centres. Newmarket which boasts a large, modern plaza, has emerged as the principal shopping centre of northern York County, and certainly offers more in the way of central goods than its size implies. However, the primary reason why Bradford and Newmarket do not patronize Barrie is that both are within a 45-minute drive of Yorkdale Shopping Centre in the northern suburbs of Metropolitan Toronto. Yorkdale is one of the largest planned shopping centres in North America. It is accessible directly from the multilane expressway system focussing on Toronto; its pedestrian mall is completely enclosed and air-conditioned; and its attractions are spearheaded by branch stores of both the Timothy Eaton and Robert Simpson companies, which dominate not only the department store business of Toronto, but also the mail order trade of all Ontario.

Regarded as a single unit, the entire Barrie system is a sub-system of the central place system of Toronto. This in itself is no surprise, but it is striking that informants in the field volunteered the specific name "Yorkdale" more often than the general term "Toronto." Additional inquiries indicated that Yorkdale, at least in the case of the present study area, is currently held in greater esteem by the people of "small town Ontario" than Toronto's central business district. In fact, this is so much the case that a Toronto-based bus company puts on a "special" approximately once a month for shopping excursions to Yorkdale from Barrie, Collingwood, and other centres.

Given the importance of Yorkdale, or more generally, Toronto, as a central place, it is easy to understand why Barrie's reach is so limited to the south. From the point of view of residents of Bradford and Newmarket, there is no point in going 25 miles to Barrie when Yorkdale is less than 10 miles farther away. For northern York County, indeed, Yorkdale is so attractive and so readily accessible that even the sizeable intermediate centres of Aurora (8,791), and Richmond Hill (16,446), are usually bypassed as shopping towns.

Since Bradford and Newmarket draw some trade from villages such as Cookstown and Churchill, they qualify along with Toronto as major competitive centres of Barrie, thus limiting the extent of the Barrie central place system in the south. In contrast, Barrie's reach to the southwest is not curtailed by major competitive centres in this way. Alliston (2,884), like Bradford, lies 25 miles by road from Barrie, but the distances from Bradford and Alliston to Yorkdale are 33 and 45 miles respectively. Because of this difference in space relations, Alliston relies much more on Barrie than on Toronto, and hence is a primary tributary centre of Barrie rather than a major competitive centre.

South of Alliston, a few small centres like Beeton and Tottenham qualify in turn as primary peripheral centres in the Barrie system. Note on Figure 16 that Tottenham, the southernmost central place in Barrie's system, lies considerably closer to Toronto than the limit of Barrie's reach down the Yonge Street highway axis farther east.[9] The southerly bulge in the Barrie system west of Highway 27 results partly from the fact that Alliston, unlike Bradford, is a member of the Barrie system, and partly from the fact that residents of villages like Beeton and Tottenham are apprehensive at the thought of a drive to Toronto, and find little Alliston as busy as a town needs to be. The contrast between urban and rural attitudes in

---

[9]Yonge Street (Highway 11), was one of the earliest roads in Ontario, and was first constructed at the very end of the eighteenth century to promote settlement and the fur trade. It linked the harbour at York, now Toronto, with Lake Simcoe, whence water routes connected with Georgian Bay and the Upper Great Lakes. Today, Yonge Street connects Toronto with Northern Ontario and the West, and is paralleled south of Barrie by Highways 27 and 400 (see also Figure 22).

the few miles which separate, say, Bradford and Beeton should not be overdrawn, but it is sufficiently well marked to influence shopping habits, and hence to affect the shape of Barrie's central place system.

It is towards the west that the Barrie system extends farthest from its central city. In this direction, no town which is even half as large as Barrie occurs until one reaches Owen Sound (17,421), whose central place system adjoins that of Barrie on the west. Barrie does not have a very strong hold over the far western portion of its system, as shown by the number of primary peripheral centres in this area on Figure 16. This western area is brought into the Barrie system through the dependence of the villages of Singhampton, Glen Huron, and others upon Collingwood (8,385), and Creemore (850), just as the southernmost portion of the system is created by the reliance of Beeton and Tottenham upon Alliston.

While the limits of the Barrie system to the north and south of the central city are set by the presence of major competitive centres, it is noteworthy that no centres of this type lie to the west or southwest. In these directions, it happens that there is no centre outside the system whose size and location enable it to attract customers from places which regularly patronize Barrie. Towns which appear to be potential major competitive centres of Barrie, such as Meaford (3,834), and Orangeville (4,593), turn out on investigation to be so small and distant in relation to Barrie that they rank among the latter's non-competitive centres. This lack of major competitive centres accounts for the greater reach of Barrie towards the west and southwest, but the preponderance of primary peripheral centres in these directions indicates that the extension in distance of Barrie's influence is accompanied by a sacrifice of some of its strength.

Despite the fact that Owen Sound is a smaller central place than Barrie, the Owen Sound system covers the larger territory In part, this results from the fact that the entire Bruce Peninsula is tributary to Owen Sound, but it also reflects the fact that the influence of Owen Sound is even less restricted by major competitive centres than that of Barrie. Owen Sound's major competitive centres are actually more numerous than those of Barrie, but they are smaller and more distant from the central city. In consequence, as Figure 17 indicates, the Owen Sound system extends 30 miles and more from its central city in all directions, except where the waters of Lake Huron and Georgian Bay intervene.

Mention has already been made of the sparse population in the Bruce Peninsula, and of the fact that over 80 per cent of the people in the Owen Sound system reside south of the central city. Although the Bruce Peninsula is linked to Manitoulin Island by ferry in summer, the emptiness of these northern localities has prevented the growth in the peninsula of a large town which could function as a major competitive centre of Owen Sound. Moreover, while the distance from Tobermory, at the tip of the peninsula, to Owen Sound is 68 miles, the distance from Tobermory to Sudbury, north of Georgian Bay, is 120 miles; and to this road distance of 120 miles must be added the inconvenience of the ferry crossing to South Baymouth, and the fact that the trip to Sudbury cannot be made at all in winter, when the ferry does not operate. Taken together, these factors explain why the entire Bruce Peninsula looks south rather than north, and falls within the central place system of Owen Sound.

Turning to the southern portion of the Owen Sound system, the boundary is seen on Figure 17 to be patrolled by a series of major competitive centres from Kincardine to Collingwood. Not shown on Figure 17, but equally important as major competitive centres of Owen Sound, are the large cities of London (181, 283), Kitchener-Waterloo (154, 864), and Guelph (41, 767), farther south. All three of these cities exert noteworthy influence in this northwestern part of Southern Ontario, and all three draw some trade from Owen Sound itself as well as from other centres in the Owen Sound system.

The southern boundary of the Owen Sound system is in general closely approximated by a circle of 30 miles radius centred on Owen Sound (Figure 17). The only conspicuous exception to this statement is the southeasterly protrusion of the system boundary along Highway 10 towards Orangeville. Corbetton, at the extremity of this protrusion, lies over 40 miles from Owen Sound. Inquiries in the field reveal that two factors account for this protrusion. First, there is the fact that major competitive centres of Owen Sound are weaker in this sector than elsewhere; Shelburne, 53 miles from Owen Sound, has a population of only 1, 239, and Orangeville, still more distant, a population of 4, 593. Secondly, there is the existence of Highway 10 itself, originally a "colonization road" opened through the bush in the mid-nineteenth century to encourage settlement. It happens that the line of this road cuts diagonally across the rectangular survey pattern of this part of Ontario, as can be seen on the appropriate modern topographic map sheet. [10] Residents of the Corbetton and Dundalk vicinity are thus provided with a paved route into Owen Sound which is much more direct than the regular survey roads allow.

The Owen Sound system occupies most of Bruce and Grey Counties, together with a small part of Dufferin County in the southeast (Figure 17). The Barrie system occupies almost all of the southern two-thirds of Simcoe County, together with small portions of Dufferin and Grey Counties in the west (Figure 16). By combining the populations of the appropriate Townships and incorporated centres, and estimating the figures for fractions of Townships where necessary, it is found that the total population within the Barrie system is approximately 83,500. The Owen Sound system is slightly less populous, with 72,000 as the approximate total. [11] The Barrie system contains 64 central places, of which 44 are primary tributary centres and 19 are primary peripheral centres of the central city. In the Owen Sound system, there are 83 central places, including 77 primary tributary centres and 5 primary peripheral centres.

SOURCES OF CENTRALITY DATA

With the central place systems now identified, the next step is to make an inventory of all establishments performing central functions in the towns and villages which the systems contain. This inventory is based upon a variety of published business directories, supplemented by extensive field checking.

The most complete published source for the retail and service businesses in places is the reference book issued six times a year by Dun and Bradstreet of Canada Limited, the Canadian branch of the well-known American credit rating agency. [12]

10 See especially Sheet 41A, Bruce, at 1:250,000.

[11] 1961 Census of Canada, Vol. I, Part 1, Table 7.

[12] Dun and Bradstreet of Canada Limited, Reference Book: November, 1965 (Toronto: Dun and Bradstreet). This work is not available in public libraries, but may be consulted at the regional Dun and Bradstreet office, in this case, Toronto.

This book lists the communities in each Province alphabetically, and gives the County in which each entry is situated, so it is a simple matter to extract the places in any particular study area. Dun and Bradstreet's listing of places is very thorough, but not quite exhaustive. Twelve of the 147 central places in the present study area were not listed in the reference book, but none of these twelve has more than three business establishments.

Dun and Bradstreet attempt to include in their directory every industrial and commercial establishment which is currently in business. Each firm is classified according to the four-digit Standard Industrial Classification (SIC) code, a system which was originally developed in the United States to facilitate the presentation of business statistics on a uniform basis. The use of the SIC code makes it possible to extract, from the Dun and Bradstreet list for each place, only those business types which qualify as central functions.

Each function (that is, each different SIC code number) listed by Dun and Bradstreet was examined to see whether that type of firm existed primarily to serve the final consumer. Functions satisfying this condition were accepted as central functions, and were included in the inventory. In practice, this meant that all firms classified in the SIC code under "Retail Trade" were included in the study, together with certain types classified under "Finance and Real Estate" and "Services." For a few firms in the reference book, two SIC code numbers are given; this represents the presence of an important "second line." In such cases, the establishment was recorded twice, once under each function. All establishments were separately tallied, so that the resulting tabulations showed not only the number of central functions in each place, but also the number of establishments of each function.

Field experience subsequently revealed that the Dun and Bradstreet data were remarkably complete in the case of "Retail Trade" firms, but somewhat less trustworthy in the "Finance and Real Estate" and "Services" categories. Firms of the latter two types were thus made a principal target of field observation. Data were also gathered from all the local telephone directories, care being taken to check the latter against the Dun and Bradstreet lists to avoid counting the same establishment twice. It is worth noting that telephone directories are a good source of information on service firms, but a very poor source for <u>retail</u> functions. One reason for this is that retailers are much less inclined to have themselves entered in the classified "yellow pages" than firms providing professional or semi-professional services. Another reason is that "physician," "dentist," and many other professions are listed as such following the individual's name in the alphabetical section of the directory, while retailers are referred to, if at all, in general terms such as "merchant," or simply "store."

In addition to the data gathered from Dun and Bradstreet and the local telephone directories, specialized and highly reliable sources were consulted for the locations of post offices, public libraries, County seats, daily and weekly newspapers, banks, beer and liquor stores, doctors, and general hospitals.[13] With the exception of banks, none of these important central functions is included in the Dun and Bradstreet reference book. However, as far as could be determined in the field, the sources used for information on these functions were absolutely complete and correct.

The final tabulations showed that the 147 central places in the two systems under investigation performed a total of 74 different central functions. Table 4 lists these 74 functions in their overall order of decreasing ubiquity; that is, the functions are ranked by the number of central places in which they occur in the study area as a whole. It should be noted that the functions change their order slightly when ranked by decreasing ubiquity for the two systems separately.

In making this inventory, each establishment was normally recorded under one heading only. For example, a hay, grain, and feed dealer who sold a few rakes and shovels was recorded only under "hay, grain, and feed," and not also under "hardware." However, there were three exceptions to this rule.

---

[13] The sources are as follows, with the appropriate functions noted in parentheses where not readily apparent: Canada, Postmaster General, <u>List of Post Offices with Revenues for the Year Ended March 31, 1961</u> (Ottawa: Queen's Printer, 1961); <u>Canadian Almanac and Directory for 1967</u> (Toronto: Copp Clark) (public libraries); Ontario, Department of Municipal Affairs, <u>1967 Municipal Directory</u> (Toronto: Ontario Department of Municipal Affairs) (County seats); <u>Canadian Advertising Rates and Data</u>, August, 1967 (Toronto: Maclean-Hunter) (daily and weekly newspapers); <u>Bank Directory of Canada</u>, July, 1966 (Toronto: Houstons Standard Publications); <u>Brewers Retail Store Directory, 1966-67</u> (Toronto: Brewers Warehousing Company); <u>LCBO Price List</u>, May, 1966 (Toronto: Liquor Control Board of Ontario) (liquor stores); <u>Canadian Medical Directory, 1967</u> (Toronto: Current Publications), sec. 2, "Physicians by Town," pp. 513-627; <u>Canadian Hospital Directory, 1966</u> (Toronto: Canadian Hospital Association).

TABLE 4. CENTRAL FUNCTIONS IN THE STUDY AREA

Type of Store or Service	Number of Places in which this Function Occurs	Type of Store or Service	Number of Places in which this Function Occurs
General store	127	Simpson-Sears mail order office	11
Gas station	87	General hospital	11
Post office	83	Automobile accessory store	10
Grocery store	49		
Restaurant	39	Billiards	9
Hardware store	37	Florist	8
Bank	36	Sporting goods store	8
Insurance agency	33	Family clothing store	7
Lumber, bldg. supplies, fuels	31	Children's and infants' wear store	7
Beauty salon	30		
Specialized automobile repair	30	Cinema	6
Drugstore (with pharmacist)	29	Photography studio	6
Plumbing, heating, air-conditioning	27	Eaton's mail order office	6
Hay, grain and feed dealer	26	Chiropractor	6
Furniture, appliances	26	Optometrist	6
Physician	25	Monument sales	6
Farm machinery	24	Finance company	5
Funeral parlour	23	Stationery, office supplies	5
New car dealership	22	Chain 5¢ and 10¢ store	5
Retail bakery	21	Antique dealer	4
Weekly newspaper	21	Dairy store	4
Real estate agency	19	Fresh fruit and vegetable store	3
Variety store	19	Millinery store	3
Fresh meat store	18	Camera store	3
Women's ready-to-wear clothing	18	Chinaware store	2
Lawyer's office	17	Furrier	2
Gifts, novelties, souvenirs	16	Bookstore	2
Men's and boys' clothing	16	Music store	2
Dentist	15	Daily newspaper	2
Veterinarian	15	Public library	2
Jewelry store	15	County seat	2
Beer store	15	Trust company	2
Liquor store	14	Car rental agency	2
Painting, decorating	14	Piano tuner	2
Bowling lanes	14	Hearing aid centre	2
Family shoe store	13	Candy store	1
Laundry, dry cleaning	12	Women's accessories store	1
		Garden supplies centre	1
		Men's shoe store	1

First, as noted above, establishments entered in the Dun and Bradstreet reference book with two SIC code numbers were recorded under both the functions indicated. Secondly, so-called "combination" beer and liquor stores were recorded under both

125

"beer" and "liquor." These stores occur in a few localities where the Ontario Government, which controls the sale of all beer and liquor, has decided to combine a beer outlet and a liquor outlet under the same roof. Finally, an establishment was entered under two headings if it performed two distinct activities which commonly existed as single functions in other establishments. A particularly quaint example is the combination of furniture sales and funeral directing in a single firm; this dates from a time when retailers of wood products expanded from the sale of coffins to the complete business of undertaking. Other examples of dual-function establishments are the insurance agent who also deals in real estate, and the general store which also houses the post office in most small centres.

The mail order offices of Simpson-Sears and Eaton's, the two major Toronto department store companies, are considered sufficiently distinctive in the Ontario retailing scene to be separately enumerated. Similarly, chain stores operated by the four firms of Kresge, Stedman, Woolworth, and Zeller are placed together as "chain 5¢ and 10¢ stores," and separated from the "variety store" group. In the field, it is clear that the outlets of these four companies are entirely different in quality from the stores in the "variety store" category, even though both come under the same SIC code number. Chain 5¢ and 10¢ stores are commonly a major factor in attracting shoppers from out of town, which is certainly not true of the lower quality variety store.

Certain consumer-oriented functions have deliberately been excluded from the study on the grounds that they are not integral parts of the central place systems. Hotels and motels, which cater primarily to tourists and commercial travellers, were omitted.[14] Licensed drinking places were excluded because they are banned by law in several municipalities, and hence their distribution is not entirely a reflection of economic factors. Churches and schools, while present in many nucleated centres, are also found scattered across the countryside in iso-

---

[14]It is true that hotels contain dining rooms, and the latter might have been added to the total number of "restaurants" in the inventory. On the other hand, if this type of disaggregation were carried to its logical conclusion, analysis of the entire retail economy would have to be attempted at the level of the individual good. As explained in chap. iv, however, the relative centrality of places is adequately expressed by using the central function, rather than the individual good, as the basic unit of analysis.

lation; like beverage rooms, their distribution does not primarily reflect economic factors, and they were accordingly omitted. The same applies to Township arenas and community halls, which often stand in splendid isolation along rural routes near the geometric centres of Townships. Finally, no record was made of ephemeral purveyors of honey, fishing licenses, and dew worms, whose crudely lettered signs appear along the highways at the appropriate times of the year.

One common central function is regrettably absent from Table 4, namely the barber shop. Neither Dun and Bradstreet nor the telephone directories were of any help in the case of this function, and no specialized directory of barbers could be found. The resources for fieldwork were too limited to permit exhaustive first-hand enumeration of barber shops, and it has accordingly been thought best to omit this function entirely.

For most of the central places in the study area, the data obtained from published sources have been thoroughly checked in the field. There is no doubt that the sources described above are highly reliable, since only in a few cases was it necessary to adjust the inventory on the basis of the fieldwork. On the other hand, the published sources are not strictly contemporaneous, and the field checking was not entirely exhaustive, and hence no claim is made that the data are infallible. It can be said, however, that any errors which may be present are small enough to have a negligible effect on the remainder of the analysis.

AN ANALYSIS OF CENTRALITY

Calculation of Functional Indices
The centrality data for each of the two central place systems were arranged in a table in which the rows were central places and the columns were central functions. The places were ranked by their populations, starting with the largest, and the functions were ranked by decreasing ubiquity, starting with the function occurring in the greatest number of central places in the system. This arrangement facilitates the handling of the data in general, and ranking the places by population is also a prereq-

uisite for the calculation of thresholds, discussed in the follow-ing chapter.[15]

Treating each system as a separate unit, the raw data were then converted to functional indices, using the method proposed by Davies and described earlier.[16] The first stage in this method is the calculation of the location coefficients of individ-ual functions, and these are shown for the two systems in Tables 5 and 6. These tables also show the order of decreasing ubiq-uity of the functions. In both systems, the most ubiquitous func-tion is the general store, which occurs in 54 of the 64 centres in the Barrie system, and 73 of the 83 centres in the Owen Sound system. However, in both cases, the function with the lowest location coefficient is the gas station, since this function is represented by the greatest total number of establishments.

The centrality of each centre is obtained by multiplying the number of establishments of each function in the centre by the appropriate location coefficient. To take one example, the vil-lage of Creemore in the Barrie system scores 1.23 x 3 = 3.69 for its three general stores; 0.77 x 3 = 2.31 for its three gas stations; 2.63 x 1 = 2.63 for its post office; and so forth. These scores are summed to give the final functional index, or total centrality, of each centre. For Creemore, the functional index is 174.20.

Tables 7 and 8 show the centres in the two systems ranked according to their functional indices. The numbers of functions and establishments in the centres, and their populations and annual postal revenues, are also shown for comparison. A check on the accuracy of the functional index calculations is provided by the fact that the sum of these indices equals 100 times the number of different functions in the system. This follows from the fact that each different function, by definition, contributes a centrality score of 100 to the system as a whole. In the present case, the Barrie and Owen Sound systems contain

---

[15]Population data for incorporated centres were obtained from the 1961 Census of Canada Vol. I, Part 1, Table 7. In the case of unincorporated centres, populations were taken from the 1961 Census special report, Bulletin SP-4: Unincorporated Villages. This report does not include nucleated places of less than 50 people, and the populations of the latter were therefore taken from the Dun and Bradstreet reference book. In these cases, the figures are known to be estimates. For some very small hamlets, even the Dun and Bradstreet reference book gives no figure.

[16]Wayne K. D. Davies, "Centrality and the Central Place Hierarchy," Urban Studies, Vol. 4 (1967), 61-79.

TABLE 5. BARRIE SYSTEM: LOCATION COEFFICIENTS OF CENTRAL FUNCTIONS

Function	No. of Places	No. of Establish- ments	Location Coefficient
General store	54	81	1.23
Gas station	42	130	0.77
Post office	38	38	2.63
Restaurant	22	81	1.23
Grocery store	22	80	1.25
Beauty salon	16	61	1.64
Bank	16	27	3.70
Hardware store	15	31	3.23
Lumber, bldg. supplies	14	43	2.33
Hay, grain and feed	14	20	5.00
Insurance agency	13	83	1.20
Automobile repair	13	29	3.45
Drugstore	13	26	3.85
Fresh meat store	12	16	6.25
Real estate agency	10	58	1.72
Plumbing, heating	10	36	2.78
Physician	9	72	1.39
Furniture, appliances	9	39	2.56
Farm machinery	9	22	4.55
Painting, decorating	8	18	5.56
Gifts, novelties	8	13	7.69
Retail bakery	8	12	8.33
Weekly newspaper	8	8	12.50
Lawyer's office	7	35	2.86
New car dealership	7	32	3.13
Dentist	7	24	4.17
Women's ready-to-wear	7	20	5.00
Funeral parlour	7	9	11.11
Variety store	7	9	11.11
Family shoe store	6	11	9.09
Beer store	6	7	14.29
Liquor store	6	7	14.29
Men's and boys' clothing	5	15	6.67
Laundry, dry cleaning	5	13	7.69
Veterinarian	5	10	10.00
Florist	5	8	12.50
Finance company	4	18	5.56
Jewelry store	4	12	8.33
Family clothing store	4	8	12.50
Cinema	4	7	14.29
Bowling lanes	4	6	16.67
Children's wear store	4	4	25.00
Simpson-Sears office	4	4	25.00
Antique dealer	4	4	25.00
Auto accessory store	3	9	11.11

TABLE 5—(continued)

Function	No. of Places	No. of Establish- ments	Location Coefficient
Chiropractor	3	7	14.29
Monument sales	3	7	14.29
Sporting goods store	3	6	16.67
Optometrist	3	6	16.67
Photography studio	3	5	20.00
Billiards	3	4	25.00
Fresh fruit and vegetables	3	3	33.33
General hospital	3	3	33.33
Eaton's order office	3	3	33.33
Chinaware store	2	4	25.00
Chain 5¢ and 10¢ store	2	4	25.00
Stationery store	2	3	33.33
Car rental agency	1	6	16.67
Camera store	1	4	25.00
Trust company	1	3	33.33
Music store	1	2	50.00
Candy store	1	2	50.00
Men's shoe store	1	2	50.00
Hearing aid centre	1	2	50.00
Dairy store	1	1	100.00
Millinery store	1	1	100.00
Furrier	1	1	100.00
Bookstore	1	1	100.00
Garden supplies	1	1	100.00
Daily newspaper	1	1	100.00
County seat	1	1	100.00
Piano tuner	1	1	100.00
Public library	1	1	100.00

respectively 73 and 68 different functions, giving 7,300 and 6,800 as the respective total centrality scores.

Testing for Hierarchical Structuring

The functional indices listed in Tables 7 and 8 must now be analyzed by the simultaneous application of the two criteria of discrete stratification of centrality and interstitial placement of orders. The second of these criteria is unique in that it cannot be translated into objective numerical terms for the purposes of empirical work; it can be expressed only as a requirement that the spatial pattern of central places must "strongly resemble" one or other of the theoretical models earlier de-

TABLE 6. OWEN SOUND SYSTEM: LOCATION
COEFFICIENTS OF CENTRAL FUNCTIONS

Function	No. of Places	No. of Establishments	Location Coefficient
General store	73	114	0.88
Gas station	45	133	0.75
Post office	45	45	2.22
Grocery store	27	77	1.30
Hardware store	22	39	2.56
Insurance agency	20	70	1.43
Bank	20	28	3.57
Restaurant	17	61	1.64
Furniture, appliances	17	47	2.13
Lumber, bldg. supplies	17	42	2.38
Plumbing, heating	17	37	2.70
Automobile repair	17	28	3.57
Physician	16	68	1.47
Drugstore	16	28	3.57
Funeral parlour	16	20	5.00
New car dealership	15	37	2.70
Farm machinery	15	29	3.45
Beauty salon	14	70	1.43
Retail bakery	13	20	5.00
Weekly newspaper	13	13	7.69
Hay, grain and feed	12	17	5.88
Variety store	12	15	6.67
Men's and boys' clothing	11	24	4.17
Women's ready-to-wear	11	22	4.55
Jewelry store	11	18	5.56
Lawyer's office	10	28	3.57
Veterinarian	10	12	8.33
Bowling lanes	10	11	9.09
Real estate agency	9	29	3.45
Beer store	9	9	11.11
Dentist	8	20	5.00
Liquor store	8	8	12.50
General hospital	8	8	12.50
Gifts, novelties	8	8	12.50
Laundry, dry cleaning	7	12	8.33
Family shoe store	7	11	9.09
Auto accessory store	7	11	9.09
Simpson-Sears office	7	7	14.29
Painting, decorating	6	10	10.00
Fresh meat store	6	8	12.50
Billiards	6	7	14.29
Sporting goods store	5	8	12.50
Optometrist	3	9	11.11
Photography studio	3	7	14.29
Chiropractor	3	6	16.67

TABLE 6—(continued)

Function	No. of Places	No. of Establish- ments	Location Coefficient
Family clothing store	3	4	25.00
Florist	3	4	25.00
Children's wear store	3	4	25.00
Chain 5¢ and 10¢ store	3	4	25.00
Dairy store	3	4	25.00
Eaton's order office	3	3	33.33
Monument sales	3	3	33.33
Stationery store	3	3	33.33
Cinema	2	5	20.00
Camera store	2	3	33.33
Millinery store	2	2	50.00
Finance company	1	11	9.09
Bookstore	1	3	33.33
Piano tuner	1	3	33.33
Furrier	1	2	50.00
Car rental agency	1	2	50.00
Hearing aid centre	1	2	50.00
Trust company	1	1	100.00
Daily newspaper	1	1	100.00
Public library	1	1	100.00
County seat	1	1	100.00
Music store	1	1	100.00
Women's accessories store	1	1	100.00

scribed.[17] Because of the flexibility of this requirement, this crucial stage of the analysis involves an element of trial and error. In practice, the best procedure is mentally to put the central places, starting with the largest, one by one on an imaginary map, keeping one eye on this map for evidence of spatial patterning reminiscent of the models, and the other eye on the ranked functional indices for evidence of plateaus of functional complexity. In this way, simultaneity in the application of the two criteria is ensured, thereby greatly lessening the chance of an arbitrary classification of centres. Needless to say, familiarity with the study area facilitates the application of the criteria, since the researcher by this stage of the analysis is likely to have a "possibly valid" classification in mind.

A glance at Tables 7 and 8 shows that both Barrie and Owen Sound stand well above all other centres in terms of centrality. This suggests that each central city forms a distinct hierarch-

[17]See the discussion of this point in chap. iv above.

TABLE 7. BARRIE SYSTEM: FUNCTIONAL INDICES AND RELATED DATA

Place	Functional Index	No. of Functions	No. of Establish-ments	Population (1961)	Annual Postal Revenue (Dollars)
Barrie	3,425.11	69	501	21,169	272,478
Collingwood	1,237.88	53	194	8,385	75,024
Alliston	794.92	51	122	2,884	31,451
Stayner	278.87	36	78	1,671	17,053
Elmvale	272.07	33	53	957	11,376
Wasaga Beach	216.56	23	56	431	6,910
Creemore	174.20	30	40	850	7,314
Beeton	98.73	18	22	810	6,729
Cookstown	87.28	18	27	1,025	5,612
Tottenham	67.52	15	22	778	4,734
Angus	65.82	16	31	1,180	7,785
Stroud	50.61	12	22	202	5,986
Camp Borden	50.04	10	13	1,000	28,922
Belle Ewart	39.21	5	5	364	1,673
Oro Station	33.17	5	8	100	1,787
Craighurst	33.08	5	5	56	357
Midhurst	28.70	3	4	340	
Oakview Beach	26.57	4	4	646	
Lefroy	23.75	8	12	366	2,624
Minesing	19.21	4	5	117	715
Shanty Bay	17.86	5	10	351	2,123
Feversham	17.79	6	7	151	1,407
Painswick	16.66	6	6	147	1,629
Everett	15.95	8	9	426	1,434
Thornton	14.57	6	7	260	1,608
Hillsdale	11.89	5	6	255	916
New Lowell	11.56	4	7	203	2,390
Singhampton	11.14	5	7	138	930
Duntroon	10.64	5	5	67	1,023
Nottawa	10.63	4	7	272	1,597
Mansfield	10.40	4	5	53	709
Phelpston	10.08	4	6	118	526
Churchill	9.63	4	4	173	854
Ivy	9.55	2	2	150	
Maxwell	8.27	4	6	89	713
Sunnidale Corners	6.68	4	4		
Woodland Beach	6.33	3	3	50	
Rosemont	5.86	4	4	100	612
Anten Mills	5.78	2	2	150	
Glen Huron	5.77	2	2	100	
Barclay	4.77	3	5		
Badjeros	4.63	3	3	50	564
Guthrie	4.31	2	5	146	
Glencairn	3.86	2	2	116	927
Honeywood	3.86	2	2	98	692

TABLE 7—(continued)

Place	Functional Index	No. of Functions	No. of Establishments	Population (1961)	Annual Postal Revenue (Dollars)
Lisle	3.86	2	2	219	1,062
Loretto	3.86	2	2		801
Big Bay Point	3.71	3	3	100	
Edenvale	2.77	2	3		
Dalston	2.48	2	2	63	
Edgar	2.46	2	2	100	
Baxter	2.00	2	2	103	
Brentwood	2.00	2	2		
Redickville	2.00	2	2	50	
Utopia	2.00	2	2	50	
Colgan	1.25	1	1	110	
Fergusonvale	1.25	1	1		
Allenwood	1.23	1	1		
Avening	1.23	1	1	51	
Crossland	1.23	1	1		
Egbert	1.23	1	1	25	
Langman	1.23	1	1		
Terra Nova	1.23	1	1	70	
Lamers Corners	0.77	1	1		

Data on functions and establishments are from the sources described in the text, supplemented by field observations. Population figures are from the 1961 Census of Canada or, in the case of very small centres, from Dun and Bradstreet. Data on postal revenues are from List of Post Offices with Revenues for the Year Ended March 31, 1961.

ical order in its own system. However, consideration of a single centre in each system is hardly a basis for seeking spatial regularities, and so the process of adding centres to the imaginary map is continued, a watchful eye being kept on the functional index values.

In Table 7, there is a strong suggestion that Collingwood and Alliston together might form a discrete order, and the same applies to the group of seven centres from Meaford down to Markdale in Table 8. Figures 18 and 19 show the distribution of these centres in map form. On both maps, the even spacing of the central places is notable. Barrie, Collingwood, and Alliston form an acute-angled triangle, and the positions of Collingwood and Alliston seem ideal from the point of view of serving the parts of the system most distant from the central city. A triangular arrangement is equally evident in the Owen Sound system, and here two further observations may be made.

TABLE 8. OWEN SOUND SYSTEM: FUNCTIONAL INDICES AND RELATED DATA

Place	Functional Index	No. of Functions	No. of Establish- ments	Population (1961)	Annual Postal Revenue (Dollars)
Owen Sound	3,013.88	66	417	17,421	236,593
Meaford	502.27	45	89	3,834	45,862
Wiarton	390.71	40	82	2,138	21,037
Port Elgin	388.36	40	76	1,632	18,341
Durham	383.92	40	77	2,180	18,729
Chesley	378.75	41	64	1,697	13,483
Southampton	266.73	32	55	1,818	15,392
Markdale	257.55	33	56	1,090	14,032
Dundalk	173.08	32	47	852	10,139
Thornbury	139.62	28	39	1,097	9,129
Paisley	125.68	26	41	759	7,400
Flesherton	92.96	21	29	515	6,998
Tara	81.51	18	26	481	5,087
Tobermory	56.28	12	16	363	4,513
Lions Head	53.82	12	20	416	5,512
Chatsworth	48.69	15	22	419	4,715
Clarksburg	40.05	13	15	404	5,590
Sauble Beach	37.02	7	15	73	
Elmwood	34.52	10	13	357	3,492
Hepworth	26.96	8	13	358	2,930
Cargill	26.38	8	10	231	1,508
Chepstow	22.76	5	7	135	831
Ceylon	15.76	4	4	95	553
Williamsford	14.47	6	7	213	848
Shallow Lake	14.31	6	8	340	1,166
Holland Centre	13.62	5	7	72	663
Pinkerton	12.11	5	5	65	626
Varney	10.58	5	6	100	599
Desboro	10.49	5	7	160	1,413
Allenford	10.35	5	8	209	1,732
Eugenia	9.19	4	5	88	389
Berkeley	8.18	4	6	116	453
Eden Grove	7.42	4	4	150	329
Kemble	7.42	4	4	50	423
Heathcote	6.55	3	3	101	853
Kimberley	6.38	3	4	71	484
Walters Falls	6.36	3	4	140	665
Woodford	5.95	3	4	61	
Balmy Beach	5.88	1	1		
Priceville	5.87	4	4	141	818
Ferndale	5.69	3	5		
North Bruce	5.48	3	5		510
Dornoch	5.33	2	3	50	
Ravenna	4.73	3	4	150	509
Dobbinton	4.40	3	3	125	562

TABLE 8—(continued)

Place	Functional Index	No. of Functions	No. of Establish- ments	Population (1961)	Annual Postal Revenue (Dollars)
Park Head	3.98	2	3	58	446
Proton Station	3.85	3	3	53	801
Balaclava	3.57	1	1	75	
Bognor	3.10	2	2	55	233
Corbetton	3.10	2	2	89	959
Stokes Bay	3.10	2	2	142	977
Oliphant	3.06	2	3	30	
Dunkeld	2.39	2	2		
Duncan	2.18	2	2		
Rocklyn	1.76	1	2	59	
Annan	1.63	2	2	150	
Arkwright	1.63	2	2	100	
Clavering	1.63	2	2	75	
Jackson	1.63	2	2		
Keady	1.63	2	2	75	
Kilsyth	1.63	2	2	76	
Rockford	1.63	2	2		
Wolseley	1.63	2	2		
Alvanley	1.50	1	2		
Miller Lake	1.30	1	1	67	
Pike Bay	1.30	1	1		
Adamsville	0.88	1	1		
Allan Park	0.88	1	1		
Blantyre	0.88	1	1		
Burgoyne	0.88	1	1	121	
Chippawa Hill	0.88	1	1	100	
Colpoys Bay	0.88	1	1	105	
Dyers Bay	0.88	1	1	100	
East Linton	0.88	1	1		
Goring	0.88	1	1		
Leith	0.88	1	1	141	
Mar	0.88	1	1	20	
Marmion	0.88	1	1		
Oxenden	0.88	1	1	55	
Peabody	0.88	1	1		
Purple Valley	0.88	1	1	25	
Rocky Saugeen	0.88	1	1		
Springmount	0.75	1	1		

Data on functions and establishments are from the sources described in the text, supplemented by field observations. Population figures are from the 1961 Census of Canada or, in the case of very small centres, from Dun and Bradstreet. Data on postal revenues are from List of Post Offices with Revenues for the Year Ended March 31, 1961.

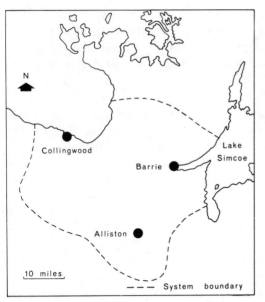

Figure 18. Barrie System: The Three Highest Ranking Centres

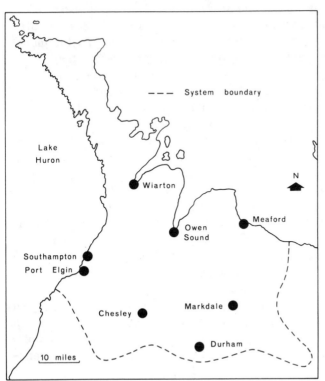

Figure 19. Owen Sound System: The Eight Highest Ranking Centres

First, extreme sparseness of population accounts for the lack of any large centre in the Bruce Peninsula north of Wiarton. Secondly, Southampton and Port Elgin may be regarded as a "twinned centre," since their central business districts are only four miles apart, and they function as a single node in the settlement pattern.

The triangular pattern of centres is strikingly maintained when the towns on Figures 18 and 19 are shown on the same map, and when certain other towns beyond the boundaries of the present systems are included. The result is shown in Figure 20. The selection of centres outside the two systems is necessarily arbitrary, but is defended on two grounds. First, all of the places chosen are comparable in functional complexity to those mapped within the two systems. Secondly, they include only the largest towns in the area covered by the map.

Figure 20 shows that Walkerton and Hanover, lying just outside the Owen Sound system, have been grouped together as twinned centres like Southampton and Port Elgin farther north. Besides these towns, the study area contains four pairs of smaller centres which are regarded as single nodes. In all cases, the twinning is defended on the grounds that the members of each pair are significantly closer together than is normal for their size. The additional twinned centres, and the distances separating their members, are Thornbury-Clarksburg (1 mile), Hepworth-Shallow Lake (2 miles), Cargill-Chepstow (4 miles), and Angus-Camp Borden (4 miles).

The triangular lattice pattern so evident on Figure 20 will be recognized as a basic feature of all Christallerian central place models, and it is encouraging to discover this pattern in an empirical study. It might be thought that the triangles outlined on Figure 20 depend in some way upon the area's road network, but such is not the case. Indeed, from the point of view of rationalizing the arrangement of central places, it is highly significant that the triangularity of the pattern becomes apparent without any consideration of road alignments. The area's principal roads are shown on Figure 22, but it will be recalled that the area is approximately isotropic with respect to transportation. Hence, the pattern of centres on Figure 20 is no mere Spielerei, but represents a very real division of an effectively homogeneous surface into areas served by a regularly spaced network of locally dominant centres.

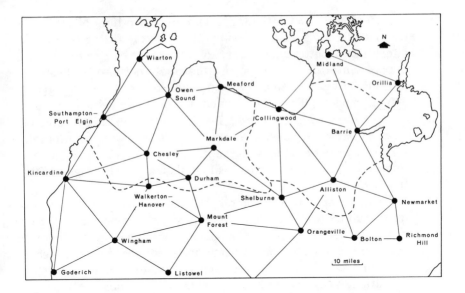

Figure 20. The Basic Lattice of Locally Dominant Centres
(Connecting lines emphasize the lattice structure)

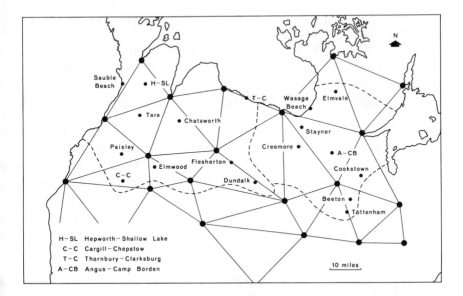

Figure 21. Interstitial Villages within the Basic Urban Lattice

139

Inevitably, in continuing down the ranked lists of functional indices in Tables 7 and 8, one anticipates the filling of the interstices in the pattern on Figure 20 by centres of a lower order. In both systems, as it happens, there is a definite tendency for interstitial centres to be located according to the Versorgungsprinzip model. This can be seen in Figure 21, which shows all centres down to Angus-Camp Borden in the Barrie system, and down to Cargill-Chepstow in the Owen Sound system. Note that the smaller centres most often lie well inside the triangles formed by the larger towns, rather than along the edges of these triangles.

Once more, it must be emphasized that two criteria are being simultaneously applied. As successively lower ranking centres from Tables 7 and 8 are added to the landscape, a point is reached in both systems at which the functional index values start to drop off sharply. In terms of the criterion of discrete stratification of centrality, this relatively sudden decline suggests a transition to a still lower order of centres. This transition must be taken into account, despite the fact that not all interstices in the previous pattern are yet filled. The functional index values, in the last analysis, represent the de facto status of central places. It has earlier been proposed that the functional indices of centres may be arbitrarily adjusted in considering the question of whether a system constitutes a perfect or an imperfect hierarchy. Such adjustment, however, is to be construed only as a means of testing a system with regard to the criterion of discrete stratification of centrality, and not as a means of achieving perfection in the interstitial placement of orders.

Hence, below the level of Angus-Camp Borden in the Barrie system, and of Cargill-Chepstow in the Owen Sound system, an order of hamlets is recognized in each of the two areas. These smallest centres are far more numerous than correspondence with the Versorgungsprinzip model requires. However, they do occur in all parts of the study area, and may be said to occupy the interstices between the larger centres. In both systems, the functional indices of these smallest places are fairly well separated from those of centres of higher rank.

While the Versorgungsprinzip pattern is readily recognizable, the study area departs from the model in several localities. For example, the triangle formed by Chesley, Kincardine, and Walkerton-Hanover contains the twinned centre of Cargill-Chepstow, instead of a single village as called for in the model. The triangle formed by Owen Sound, Meaford, and Markdale, despite its large size, contains no interstitial centre of village rank at all. Farther east, Thornbury-Clarksburg is located in accordance with the Verkehrsprinzip rather than the Versorgungsprinzip pattern. In the Barrie system, superfluous villages appear in more than one triangle. These and other anomalies are examined in the discussion of non-central-place activities.

It will be recalled that a perfect hierarchy is a system in which centres can be grouped in such a way that between-group differences in centrality are greater than, or at least equal to, within-group differences. An imperfect hierarchy, on the other hand, is a system which does not satisfy this criterion of perfection, but which can be made into a perfect hierarchy by arbitrary alteration of the functional indices of not more than 20 per cent of all centres. In the present case, application of the criteria of discrete stratification and interstitial placement leads to the tentative conclusion that both the Barrie and the Owen Sound systems are properly described as imperfect central place hierarchies.

This conclusion is tentative only in that three further criteria of hierarchical structuring remain to be considered. As it happens, all three are satisfied by both systems. On the one hand, the original tabulations of centrality data show that both systems meet the criterion of incremental baskets of goods. On the other hand, the existence of more than two orders, and of pyramidal sequences of numbers of centres in successive orders, can be verified from what has already been said.

Tables 9 and 10 show the centres in the two systems classed into orders, identified for convenience as cities, towns, villages, and hamlets.[18] In the Barrie system, the criterion of discrete stratification of centrality is satisfied if the four villages of Angus-Camp Borden, Beeton, Cookstown, and Tottenham have their functional indices raised to the level of Creemore. In the Owen Sound system, the indices of ten centres must be changed:

---

[18]As before, these terms merely serve as convenient labels for the steps in the hierarchy, and do not imply anything in regard to the legal status of the centres.

TABLE 9. BARRIE SYSTEM: HIERARCHICAL CLASSIFICATION OF CENTRES

Rank	Place	Functional Index	No. of Functions	Population (1961)
City	Barrie	3,425.11	69	21,169
Town	Collingwood	1,237.88	53	8,385
	Alliston	794.92	51	2,884
Village	Stayner	278.87	36	1,671
	Elmvale	272.07	33	957
	Wasaga Beach	216.56	23	431
	Creemore	174.20	30	850
	Angus-Camp Borden	115.86	19	2,180
	Beeton	98.73	18	810
	Cookstown	87.28	18	1,025
	Tottenham	67.52	15	778
Hamlet[1]	Stroud	50.61	12	202
	Belle Ewart	39.21	5	364
	Oro Station	33.17	5	100
	Craighurst	33.08	5	56
	Midhurst	28.70	3	340
	Oakview Beach	26.57	4	646
	Lefroy	23.75	8	366
	Minesing	19.21	4	117
	Shanty Bay	17.86	5	351
	Feversham	17.79	6	151
	Painswick	16.66	6	147
	Everett	15.95	8	426

[1] Forty additional hamlets have functional indices ranging down to a value of 0.77. See Table 7.

(1) raise Markdale to the level of Chesley;

(2) lower Thornbury-Clarksbury, Dundalk and Paisley to the level of Flesherton;

(3) raise Lions Head, Cargill-Chepstow, Hepworth-Shallow Lake, Chatsworth, Sauble Beach and Elmwood to the level of Tobermory.

In both systems, the numbers of places affected by these changes are well below 20 per cent of all centres, and the unadjusted data therefore satisfy the condition for an imperfect hierarchy.

Figure 22 shows the spatial pattern of the final classification of the centres. Strictly speaking, the Barrie and Owen Sound systems are separate entities, but there are two grounds for showing them on one map with a single legend. First, as Tables 9 and 10 indicate, the members of corresponding orders in the two systems are quite similar in terms of their functional index

TABLE 10. OWEN SOUND SYSTEM: HIERARCHICAL CLASSIFICATION OF CENTRES

Rank	Place	Functional Index	No. of Functions	Population (1961)
City	Owen Sound	3,013.88	66	17,421
Town	Southampton-Port Elgin	655.09	45	3,450
	Meaford	502.27	45	3,834
	Wiarton	390.71	40	2,138
	Durham	383.92	40	2,180
	Chesley	378.75	41	1,697
	Markdale	257.55	33	1,090
Village	Thornbury-Clarksburg	179.67	31	1,501
	Dundalk	173.08	32	852
	Paisley	125.68	26	759
	Flesherton	92.96	21	515
	Tara	81.51	18	481
	Tobermory	56.28	12	363
	Lions Head	53.82	12	416
	Cargill-Chepstow	49.14	9	366
	Chatsworth	48.69	15	419
	Hepworth-Shallow Lake	41.27	10	698
	Sauble Beach	37.02	7	73
	Elmwood	34.52	10	357
Hamlet[1]	Ceylon	15.76	4	95
	Williamsford	14.47	6	213
	Holland Centre	13.62	5	72
	Pinkerton	12.11	5	65
	Varney	10.58	5	100
	Desboro	10.49	5	160
	Allenford	10.35	5	209
	Eugenia	9.19	4	88
	Berkeley	8.18	4	116
	Eden Grove	7.42	4	150

[1]Fifty additional hamlets have functional indices ranging down to a value of 0.75. See Table 8.

values and the total numbers of functions they contain. Secondly, the area's previously noted resemblance to the Versorgungs-prinzip pattern transcends the borders of the individual systems, as shown in Figure 21. This latter fact is consistent with the idea that the two systems mapped are sub-systems of a larger system, one which may be too extensive to rely exclusively on central place connections for its identity. This notion invites attention, but lies beyond the scope of the present study. What is significant about the classification shown in Figure 22 is that, without the concept of a system of central places, it would not have been possible objectively to identify the Barrie and Owen Sound networks as hierarchical entities in the Christallerian sense.

143

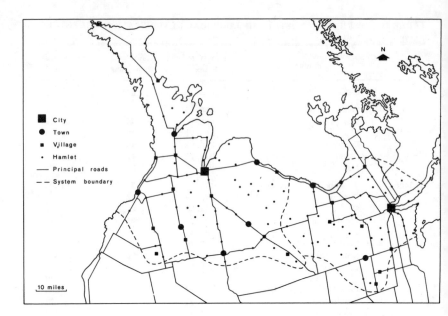

Figure 22. Hierarchical Classification of Centres

The Role of Non-Central-Place Activities

Four significant non-central-place activities are present in the study area: manufacturing, the tourist industry, wholesaling, and the training of army personnel. The quantitative influence of these activities on the centrality of places is hard to assess, but it is possible to indicate in a general way how the systems would probably appear if these activities were absent.

A crude quantitative measure of the effect of manufacturing on centrality has been devised, and may be illustrated with reference to the Barrie system. First, the estimated population of the entire system (83,513), is divided by the total centrality within the system (7,300 units), to derive an estimate of the number of people needed, in the aggregate, to give rise to one unit of centrality. The result is 11.44 persons per centrality unit. Secondly, data are obtained on the numbers of male employees in manufacturing in each centre.[19] On the grounds that

[19]Ontario, Department of Economics and Development, Industrial Directory of Municipal Data (2 vols.; Toronto: Ontario Department of Economics and Development, 1967).

144

each male employee is the head of a household of four, these figures are quadrupled to provide estimates of the total numbers of people directly supported by manufacturing in each centre. Thirdly, each of these totals is divided by 11.44 to give an estimate of the centrality score attributable to the presence of manufacturing in each centre. The functional indices of the centres in question are then adjusted accordingly.

An example will clarify the procedure. The number of male employees in manufacturing in Alliston is listed in the current Industrial Directory as 232. This is taken to represent 928 persons (232 times 4), directly dependent upon manufacturing. Dividing 928 by 11.44 gives an estimate of 81 centrality units which Alliston would not possess if it were not for the presence of manufacturing. Accordingly, it is assumed that the absence of manufacturing would mean a reduction in Alliston's functional index from 794.92 to 713.92.

In the Owen Sound system, containing 6,800 centrality units and an estimated 71,774 people, an average of 10.56 persons is required to sustain one centrality unit. The similarity between this figure and the corresponding 11.44 persons in the Barrie system is not unexpected. In general terms, the two systems are about equal in size, in degree of urbanization, and in overall socio-economic characteristics. Even so, the similarity of the two coefficients lends some support to their use, despite the roughness of the method.

Tables 11 and 12 show the results of applying the necessary adjustments to all centres in which manufacturing occurs. In the Barrie system (Table 11), a definite "tightening" of the orders is discernible; note especially the effect on Collingwood and Alliston. In the Owen Sound system (Table 12), the reduction of Thornbury-Clarksburg's centrality seems appropriate, but the same cannot be said of the changed relative positions of Markdale and Dundalk. In several respects, Dundalk is the least tractable of all centres: its location, as Figure 21 shows, is anomalous; and its nearest neighbours of town rank—Markdale and Shelburne—are among the very smallest of the centres forming the basic lattice of Figure 20. Intuitively, one suspects that the strength of Dundalk is associated with the historic importance of Highway 10 as a colonization road, promoting an initially narrow band of settlement with central places competing in a linear rather than an areal milieu. This said, it is

145

TABLE 11. BARRIE SYSTEM: FUNCTIONAL
INDICES ADJUSTED FOR MANUFACTURING

Rank	Place	Unadjusted[1] Functional Index	Adjusted Functional Index
City	Barrie	3,425.11	2,540.11
Town	Collingwood	1,237.88	616.88
	Alliston	794.92	713.92
Village	Stayner	278.87	258.87
	Elmvale	272.07	265.07
	Wasaga Beach		216.56
	Creemore	174.20	170.20
	Angus-Camp Borden		115.86
	Beeton		98.73
	Cookstown		87.28
	Tottenham	67.52	60.52
Hamlet	None of the 52 centres of hamlet rank contains manufacturing in an amount sufficient to affect the value of the functional index.[2]		

[1]Unadjusted functional indices are shown only for those
centres in which an adjustment for the presence of manufacturing is required.

[2]See Table 7 for the functional indices of hamlets.

felt best to leave the classification as it stands on Figure 22.

On the whole, the adjustments made for the presence of
manufacturing bring about a slight net improvement in the discreteness of the hierarchical orders. This is encouraging in
view of the fact that the method is exceedingly coarse. However, both systems remain as imperfect rather than perfect
hierarchies, since perfectly discrete stratification of centrality is not obtained even with the adjusted functional indices.

Turning to the tourist industry, there is no doubt that all
places in the study area except the remoter hamlets derive some
minor benefits from the passage of tourists during the summer
season. However, Wasaga Beach and Sauble Beach are the only
centres which owe a major part of their functional endowment
to the tourist trade. Many of the establishments in Wasaga
Beach, and all of those in Sauble Beach, are closed during the
winter months. In appearance, both centres are strictly beach-
oriented, and it is clear that their centrality would be deci-
mated if the flow of tourist dollars were to cease. Indeed,

146

TABLE 12.   OWEN SOUND SYSTEM: FUNCTIONAL
INDICES ADJUSTED FOR MANUFACTURING

Rank	Place	Unadjusted[1] Functional Index	Adjusted Functional Index
City	Owen Sound	3,013.88	2,302.88
Town	Southampton–Port Elgin	655.09	511.09
	Meaford	502.27	305.27
	Wiarton	390.71	384.71
	Durham	383.92	189.92
	Chesley	378.75	298.75
	Markdale	257.55	169.55
Village	Thornbury–Clarksburg	179.67	95.67
	Dundalk	173.08	171.08
	Paisley	125.68	121.68
	Flesherton	92.96	86.96
	Tara		81.51
	Tobermory		56.28
	Lions Head		53.82
	Cargill–Chepstow		49.14
	Chatsworth		48.69
	Hepworth–Shallow Lake		41.27
	Sauble Beach		37.02
	Elmwood		34.52
Hamlet	None of the 60 centres of hamlet rank contains manufacturing in an amount sufficient to affect the value of the functional index. [2]		

[1]Unadjusted functional indices are shown only for those centres in which an adjustment for the presence of manufacturing is required.

[2]See Table 8 for the functional indices of hamlets.

Sauble Beach would simply not exist as a central place, and Wasaga Beach would be no more than a hamlet. It is significant that the removal of these two centres from the village category would eliminate two of the principal locational anomalies on Figures 21 and 22. Here is a case where departures from the model are clearly the result of concentrations of non-central-place activity.

Among the larger centres, Barrie, Collingwood, Thornbury, Meaford, and especially Wiarton and Southampton–Port Elgin benefit in moderate degree from the tourist trade. It is a fortuitous coincidence that the factor which attracts tourists— coastal location—also robs most of these centres of land which would fall naturally into their umlands. It would be foolhardy to assert that the loss of centrality due to the truncated umlands is precisely balanced by the influx of tourist money, but at least it can be claimed that these two factors do tend to cancel each other out. In other words, it is at least credible that the Versorgungsprinzip model should fit these centres as well as it fits those which lie inland but receive negligible tourist trade.

Where wholesaling is concerned, data from Dun and Bradstreet show that there are 32 establishments in Barrie, 30 in Owen Sound, 12 in Collingwood, 6 in Durham, 5 in Alliston, and not more than two in any other centre.[20] Unfortunately, information on the numbers of employees in wholesaling is not available, but field inquiries revealed that practically all wholesale establishments employ less than ten persons. Using the same estimating procedure described above for manufacturing, it is clear that wholesaling has virtually no effect on the structure of either of the two hierarchies.

Finally, military training is represented in the Barrie system by Camp Borden, an army camp of some 36 square miles located 12 miles southwest of Barrie. Camp Borden's complement of military personnel fluctuates, but runs as high as 10,000, and the twinned village of Angus-Camp Borden depends almost exclusively upon the army's presence for its existence as a central place. Assuming that the military base were to disappear, and that the area it occupies were to be given over to agriculture, there would be no need for this village centre to exist. This view is reinforced by the fact that the area of the camp does not have a high agricultural potential; indeed, its broken, sandy terrain was one reason for its selection as a training ground in the first place. It is conjectured that the removal of the camp would entail the disappearance of Angus-Camp Borden, the slack being taken up by Stayner and Barrie. Once more, note on Figure 21 that this change would eliminate a major anomaly from the pattern. Here again, non-central-place activity accounts for a departure from the model.

It can be argued that the removal of Camp Borden would also entail a reduction in the centrality of Barrie itself, since personnel from the camp spend time and money in Barrie when they are on short-term leave. However, the removal of the

[20]Dun and Bradstreet of Canada Limited, Reference Book: November, 1965.

camp would not affect Barrie's status as a centre of city rank, since the limited patronage of army personnel is not sufficient to account for the centrality difference which presently exists between Barrie and the centres in the next lower order.

Having made reasonable allowances for the presence of all types of non-central-place activity, it is clear that neither the Barrie nor the Owen Sound system becomes an appreciably more perfect hierarchy than was initially determined. On the other hand, the effects of non-central-place activities do account for several of the locational anomalies on Figures 21 and 22. The remaining anomalies can be accounted for, albeit less rigorously, by considering the joint effects of abnormally important transport routes and variations in the density of purchasing power. Thus, the villages of Thornbury-Clarksburg, Flesherton, and Dundalk, which are located in accordance with the Verkehrsprinzip rather than the Versorgungsprinzip model, may be taken to reflect the early and continuing importance of the coast road and of Highway 10, both of which were in use before the adjoining Townships were fully settled. In addition, as noted earlier, the density of disposable income is lowest in this central part of the study area, and rises towards the eastern and western ends. This may help to account for the relative lack of centres of village rank in the central portion of the area, and for the absence of such centres from the insides of several of the triangles appearing on Figure 21.

There can be little doubt that the main features of the Barrie and Owen Sound central place systems correspond to a pattern which is deducible from classical central place theory. Certain departures from perfect hierarchical structuring can be rendered intelligible through an analysis of the effects of non-central-place activities. Other anomalies appear to be associated with the historic importance of certain transport lines, and with inequalities in the density of disposable income. When allowances are made for all these distorting factors, the pattern which remains would seem to differ from the Versorgungsprinzip model only by chance. It is concluded that the dismantling of the original network in this way provides an adequate explanation of the size and spacing of nucleated settlements. Moreover, it is noteworthy that this explanation is achieved through the application of criteria which have been designed to avoid, so far as possible, arbitrariness in the identi-

149

fication of orders of central places. Accordingly, the empirical methodology developed in chapter iv appears in general to be validated.

VI

Comparison and Conclusions

While the identification of the structure of a single central place system is an end in itself, the scope of the research is significantly expanded when comparisons are made possible by the study of two or more systems. For this reason two central place systems have been identified in the present study. In this chapter, certain characteristics of the two systems are compared, but it must be stressed that the real value of such work will only emerge as the body of comparative data grows larger through the identification of more individual systems.

COMPARATIVE CHARACTERISTICS
OF THE CENTRAL PLACE SYSTEMS

Variations in Hierarchical Structure
The Barrie and Owen Sound systems are alike in that they both contain four orders of central places distributed essentially in accordance with Christaller's Versorgungsprinzip model. Moreover, the distinctive triangular lattice formed by centres of town and city rank continues unbroken throughout the territory covered by both systems (Figure 20). This continuity of the basic lattice of locally dominant centres makes it possible to speak of the entire study area as being occupied by a single hierarchical structure. However, the hierarchical nature of the overall pattern is identifiable only through a synthesis of separate studies of the individual systems comprising it.

This last point is emphasized by Figure 23, in which the centres in the two systems have been combined and ranked by the numbers of different functions they contain. Functional complexity is then plotted against rank. Notice, first, that no really clear breaks are evident on this graph; indeed, breaks are not clearly marked even if the centres in the two systems are considered separately. This illustrates the fact that stratification of orders can only be identified in the context of the relative location of the centres, and not simply from a graph of this type. Secondly, note that the centres of the Barrie hierarchy tend to fill up the gaps in the Owen Sound hierarchy; or, to put it more precisely, centres in the Barrie system normally have slightly greater functional complexity than centres of corresponding rank in the Owen Sound system. This is especially true in the case of the higher orders, as may be verified by a glance at the data on functions in Tables 9 and 10. Indeed, it can be seen that the largest village in the Barrie system has more functions than the smallest town in the Owen Sound system. [1]

The smooth continuum of Figure 23 serves as a reminder that hierarchical structuring cannot be identified unless (a) one first identifies systems of central places, and (b) one then applies to these systems not only the criterion of discrete stratification of centrality, but also the criterion of interstitial placement of orders. In short, the concept of hierarchy is an inescapably spatial concept. Abstracted from location, data on centrality form an insufficient basis for conclusions regarding hierarchical structure.

The variation in hierarchical structure between the Barrie and Owen Sound systems may be examined more closely in terms of lists of the central functions which are incremental in the four orders of the two systems. To prepare these lists, it was decided to regard a function as incremental in the lowest order in which at least half of the centres possessed the function. This rule was applied to the original tabulations of data to produce

[1]Where functional indices (as opposed to numbers of functions), are concerned, the data in Tables 9 and 10 are not strictly comparable from system to system, since they are calculated on the basis of separate establishment totals. In the present case, however, direct comparison is probably justified by the strong similarity between the two systems in overall functional complexity. Not surprisingly, comparison of the functional index values in Tables 9 and 10 leads to the same observation as that made in the text.

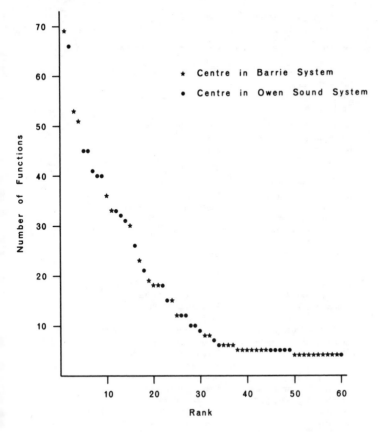

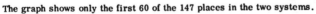

The graph shows only the first 60 of the 147 places in the two systems.

Figure 23. Barrie and Owen Sound Systems Combined:
Centres Ranked by Number of Functions

the lists in Tables 13 and 14. These tables show that three
functions are incremental at the hamlet level in the Barrie system, but that two of these functions are not incremental until
the village level in the Owen Sound system. Similarly, the
villages of the Barrie system are typified by 24 incremental
functions, 6 of which do not appear until the town level in the
Owen Sound system. Again, 29 functions are incremental in
the Barrie system's towns, but 13 of these do not appear in the

153

TABLE 13. BARRIE SYSTEM: INCREMENTAL
FUNCTIONS IN SUCCESSIVE RANKS

Rank	Incremental Functions	
Hamlet	General store	
	Gas station	
	Post office	
Village	Grocery store	Plumbing, heating
	Restaurant	Furniture, appliances
	Bank	Physician
	Beauty salon	Gifts, novelties
	Hardware store	Retail bakery
	Lumber, bldg. supplies	Weekly newspaper
	Hay, grain and feed	Funeral parlour
	Drugstore	Women's ready-to-wear
	Insurance agency	New car dealership
	Automobile repair	Variety store
	Fresh meat store	Lawyer's office
	Real estate agency	Dentist
Town	Farm machinery	Finance company
	Painting, decorating	Auto accessory store
	Family shoe store	Sporting goods store
	Liquor store	Photography studio
	Beer store	Billiards
	Men's and boys' clothing	Fresh fruit and vegetables
	Laundry, dry cleaning	General hospital
	Florist	Eaton's order office
	Veterinarian	Chiropractor
	Jewelry store	Optometrist
	Family clothing store	Monument sales
	Children's wear store	Chinaware store
	Simpson-Sears office	Stationery store
	Cinema	Chain 5¢ and 10¢ store
	Bowling lanes	
City	Dairy store	Daily newspaper
	Millinery store	Public library
	Camera store	County seat
	Furrier	Trust company
	Music store	Car rental agency
	Antique dealer	Piano tuner
	Men's shoe store	Hearing aid centre

Owen Sound system until the level of the central city itself.
Generalizing, it may be said that each order in the Barrie system contains functions which are not incremental until the next
higher order in the Owen Sound system. Significantly, no function is incremental at a lower level in the Owen Sound system
than in the Barrie system.

TABLE 14. OWEN SOUND SYSTEM:
INCREMENTAL FUNCTIONS IN SUCCESSIVE RANKS

Rank	Incremental Functions	
Hamlet	General store	
Village	Gas station	Automobile repair
	Post office	Plumbing, heating
	Grocery store	Drugstore
	Hardware store	Physician
	Insurance agency	Funeral parlour
	Bank	New car dealership
	Restaurant	Beauty salon
	Lumber, bldg. supplies	Retail bakery
	Furniture, appliances	Variety store
Town	Farm machinery	Dentist
	Weekly newspaper	General hospital
	Women's ready-to-wear	Gifts, novelties
	Men's and boys' clothing	Family shoe store
	Jewelry store	Laundry, dry cleaning
	Lawyer's office	Simpson-Sears office
	Veterinarian	Auto accessory store
	Bowling lanes	Fresh meat store
	Liquor store	Painting, decorating
	Beer store	Billiards
City	Hay, grain and feed	Camera store
	Real estate agency	Cinema
	Sporting goods store	Finance company
	Family clothing store	Trust company
	Florist	Daily newspaper
	Children's wear store	Public library
	Eaton's order office	County seat
	Chiropractor	Furrier
	Optometrist	Bookstore
	Chain 5¢ and 10¢ store	Music store
	Monument sales	Women's accessories store
	Photography studio	Car rental agency
	Stationery store	Piano tuner
	Millinery store	Hearing aid centre

This upward shift of incremental functions between the two systems appears to be correlated with the general decrease in the density of rural population from east to west across the study area (see Figure 15). A similar finding is reported by Berry, though his studies did not employ the present concept of a system of centres. In explaining the upward shift of func-tions, Berry notes that consumers appear willing to travel greater distances to obtain goods in sparsely populated areas, but that this trend is <u>more than offset</u> by the fact that the number of consumers within a given distance of a central place necessarily declines as population density decreases. Hence, as density decreases, centres at each level become unable to sustain functions whose thresholds are overtaken by the declining numbers of available consumers. Firms performing these functions can exist only in progressively higher orders, since this is the only way they can continue to satisfy their thresholds.[2]

Given this relationship between population density and incremental functions, it is possible to account for the differences in functional content between corresponding orders in the Barrie and Owen Sound hierarchies. For example, centres of village rank in the Barrie system can support, among other functions, dentists and weekly newspapers. Villages in the Owen Sound system, however, since they have fewer consumers within their range, cannot support these functions, which consequently become incremental at the town rather than the village level.

In connection with this upward shift of functions, it is interesting to recall that Berry and Garrison, in their modification of Christallerian theory, suggested that a central place network could be adapted to changes in population density through alterations in the <u>spacing</u> of the centres, rather than alterations in their functional complexity. In effect, as population density declined across space, centres of any given rank would be located progressively farther apart (Figure 9).[3] In the case of the Barrie and Owen Sound systems, the spacing of the central places does <u>not</u> increase significantly as one moves from east to west. For example, the mean airline distance from Alliston to the six surrounding centres on Figure 20 is 21 miles, while the corresponding figure for Markdale, farther west, is only 22 miles. Thus, it appears that the adjustment to decreasing population density in the study area takes the form of an upward shift of incremental functions, rather than that of an increase in the distances separating centres of equivalent rank.

---

[2]Brian J. L. Berry, <u>Geography of Market Centers and Retail Distribution</u> (Englewood Cliffs, New Jersey: Prentice-Hall, 1967), pp. 32-35.

[3]Brian J. L. Berry and William L. Garrison, "Recent Developments of Central Place Theory, " <u>Regional Science Association, Papers and Proceedings</u>, Vol. 4 (1958), 107-120.

In terms of static relations among central places, both types of adjustment are quite rational. On the other hand, when changes in population density through time are considered, it is evident that adjustment must be accomplished through changes in functional complexity, since central places cannot be shifted bodily across the countryside to bring about alterations in their spacing. It may therefore be conjectured that the basic layout of central places in the study area dates from a time when population density was more uniform than is the case today.

Turning now to another comparative aspect of the Barrie and Owen Sound hierarchies, it can be seen from Tables 9 and 10 that the two systems differ in the relative numbers of centres in successive ranks:

Barrie system: city : town : village : hamlet = 1 : 2 : 8 : 52
Owen Sound system: city : town : village : hamlet = 1 : 6 : 12 : 60

Both systems, in other words, satisfy the criterion of a pyramidal sequence of numbers. On the other hand, neither system adheres strictly to the sequence in the Versorgungsprinzip model:

Ideal sequence: city : town : village : hamlet = 1 : 2 : 6 : 18

In part, the discrepancies result from the presence of non-central-place activities in the area, and in part they merely reflect the shapes of the boundaries of the two systems. However, there is no denying that centres of hamlet rank are approximately three times as numerous as correspondence with the Versorgungsprinzip model requires. This feature is probably explained by the fact that the threshold population required to support the very limited functions of the typical hamlet is extremely small compared to the thresholds for centres of higher rank. As a result, an average of three hamlets, rather than one, can survive in each interstitial area between higher ranking centres.

A final comparative aspect of the Barrie and Owen Sound hierarchies concerns the distribution of centrality among the various orders. In both systems, as Table 15 shows, the total centrality per order decreases steadily in successively lower orders. It would be interesting to know if this type of progression holds true for all systems. No theoretical basis for predicting such a regularity comes readily to mind.

157

TABLE 15. DISTRIBUTION OF CENTRALITY BY RANKS

Rank	Percentage of Total Centrality in All Centres at Stated Rank	
	Barrie System	Owen Sound System
City	46.9	44.3
Towns	27.8	37.8
Villages	18.0	14.3
Hamlets	7.3	3.6
	100.0	100.0

Thresholds of Functions

The concept of threshold is arbitrarily defined as the minimum population required in a central place to support the performance of a particular function. As previously described, the threshold of a function is determined by first ranking all the centres in a system by population, and then identifying the population value which divides the ranked list of centres in such a way that the number of centres lacking the function above the division is equal to the number of centres possessing the function below the division. This basic rule was modified by the addition of a further condition: namely, that a threshold is only regarded as meaningful if at least half the centres above the threshold value possess the function in question. [4]

The study area as a whole contains a total of 74 different central functions, but 14 of these functions either do not exist or do not have meaningful thresholds in one or other of the two systems. Comparative data on thresholds for the remaining 60 functions are shown in Table 16. For 24 functions, this table also gives threshold values obtained by Berry and Garrison in an area north of Seattle. [5] Berry and Garrison's study involved more than 24 functions in all, but only those believed to be institutionally identical to the functions in the present study are included here for comparison.

[4]See chap. iv above. The basic rule for determining thresholds was proposed in P. Haggett and K. A. Gunawardena, "Determination of Population Thresholds for Settlement Functions by the Reed-Muench Method," Professional Geographer, Vol. 16, No. 4 (July, 1964), 6-9.

[5]Brian J. L. Berry and William L. Garrison, "The Functional Bases of the Central Place Hierarchy," Economic Geography, Vol. 34 (1958), 150.

TABLE 16. POPULATION THRESHOLDS OF FUNCTIONS

Function	Barrie System	Owen Sound System	Snohomish County
General store	20	20	
Gas station	94	75	196
Post office	100	75	
Grocery store	203	142	254
Restaurant	203	357	276
Bank	351	286	610
Beauty salon	351	416	480
Hardware store	364	211	431
Lumber, bldg. supplies	396	358	598
Insurance agency	426	231	409
Drugstore	426	363	458
Fresh meat store	431	1,665	
Plumbing, heating	794	358	
Real estate agency	794	971	384
Physician	810	410	380
Furniture, appliances	830	358	546
Farm machinery	830	410	650
Retail bakery	904	419	
Weekly newspaper	904	481	
Gifts, novelties	904	1,090	
Painting, decorating	904	1,665	
Lawyer's office	957	806	528
Funeral parlour	979	363	1,214
New car dealership	979	410	398
Women's ready-to-wear	979	759	
Dentist	979	1,094	426
Beer store	1,000	1,090	
Liquor store	1,000	1,094	
Family shoe store	1,013	1,632	
Men's and boys' clothing	1,025	759	
Laundry, dry cleaning	1,025	1,632	1,307
Florist	1,025	2,138	729
Veterinarian	1,103	806	579
Bowling lanes	1,180	852	
Simpson-Sears office	1,180	1,097	
Children's wear store	1,180	2,138	
Family clothing store	1,180	2,180	
Cinema	1,180	3,834	
Finance company	1,180	17,421	
Jewelry store	1,671	759	827
Billiards	1,671	1,665	
Photography studio	1,671	2,138	1,243
Auto accessory store	2,278	1,632	
General hospital	2,884	1,094	1,159
Sporting goods store	2,884	1,697	928

159

TABLE 16—(continued)

Function	Barrie System	Owen Sound System	Snohomish County
Monument sales	2,884	2,138	
Eaton's order office	2,884	2,159	
Chiropractor	2,884	2,180	
Chain 5¢ and 10¢ store	8,385	2,180	
Millinery store	21,169	2,180	
Camera store	21,169	2,180	
Furrier	21,169	17,421	
Music store	21,169	17,421	
Daily newspaper	21,169	17,421	
Public library	21,169	17,421	
County seat	21,169	17,421	
Trust company	21,169	17,421	
Car rental agency	21,169	17,421	
Piano tuner	21,169	17,421	
Hearing aid centre	21,169	17,421	

The Snohomish County data are taken from Berry and Garrison, "The Functional Bases of the Central Place Hierarchy," p. 150.

Table 16 shows that the thresholds of individual functions are usually lower in the Owen Sound system than in the Barrie system. In fact, this is true for 43 of the 60 functions listed. In the field, one obtains the impression that many of the establishments in Bruce and Grey Counties are operating closer to the economic margin than their counterparts farther east. Generalization may be premature, but this subjective impression is certainly supported by the statistical evidence of lower thresholds in the Owen Sound system.

On the basis of all 60 functions in Table 16, a value of 0.895 is obtained for Spearman's coefficient of rank correlation for the order of entry of functions into the two systems. Thus, while the absolute values of thresholds differ, there is a high probability that centres in the two systems containing the same number of different functions will in fact contain the same functions.

Spearman's coefficient may also be used to test the similarity of the Barrie and Owen Sound systems to the Snohomish County area studied by Berry and Garrison. Using only the 24 functions for which comparable data are available in all three

areas, the value of the coefficient for the Barrie and Owen
Sound systems drops from 0.895 to 0.822. The value when
Snohomish County is compared to the Barrie system is 0.720,
and for Snohomish County and the Owen Sound system it is
0.591. Thus, the mutual similarity of the Barrie and Owen
Sound systems remains strongly marked, but the Snohomish
County data resemble those of the Barrie area more than they
do those of the Owen Sound area.

One cannot help but wonder if metropolitan influence plays
a part here. Both Snohomish County and the Barrie system are
in close contact with metropolitan centres (Seattle and Toronto
respectively), while the Owen Sound system is more remote,
and much more rural in outlook. In addition, the Owen Sound
area has a generally lower standard of living, and it may well
be that this factor influences shopping behaviour. With considerably more data available, it might become possible to test
the hypothesis that the pattern of consumption of central goods
in an area, and hence the order of entry of central functions,
is significantly affected by proximity to a metropolitan centre.

Continuous Functional Relationships

As a general rule, one expects larger towns to have more functions, more establishments, and hence greater centrality than
smaller towns; indeed, the world would be a strange place if
this were not so. However, it is not obvious to the casual observer that certain aspects of this general trend can be expressed with moderate precision in the form of linear equations.
The empirical regularities expressed in these equations currently lack a formal theoretical explanation, but they are interesting for two reasons. First, they permit comparisons of
different central place systems to be made. Secondly, assuming they represent situations which may be termed normal, they
provide a means of isolating deviant or abnormal towns for further consideration.

In both the Barrie and Owen Sound systems, high statistical
correlations exist between (a) the numbers of central functions
in places and the logarithms of their populations, (b) the numbers of central functions and the logarithms of numbers of establishments, and (c) the numbers of central functions and the
logarithms of functional indices. These variables, and the
relevant correlation coefficients and regression equations, are

161

recorded in Table 17, and the relationships are shown graphically in Figures 24 to 29. It should be noted that these continuous functional relationships apply only to centres of village rank and above. Hamlets are too variable in composition for high correlations to be maintained, and a precedent for their exclusion is found in the work of Berry and his associates.[6]

Table 17 indicates that the equations describing each relationship are virtually identical in the two systems. This implies that the two areas have the same economic structure, at least insofar as the latter is reflected by the rates at which functions are added and establishments duplicated as town size increases. The similarity of the two areas is further emphasized by Figures 30 and 31, in which the data of both systems are combined. The correlation coefficients remain high, and the regression equations are extremely close to those obtained when the systems are treated as separate units.

Comparison of these results with those of other investigators is hampered by the fact that consistency of data and methodology cannot be guaranteed. For example, some investigators collect data for every centre in their study areas, while others use only a sample of towns. Nevertheless, a preliminary comparison is given in Table 18 for the case of the relationship between populations and numbers of functions. A high degree of correlation has been found in all studies, and the relationship is always log-linear. The regression equation derived by Thomas, in particular, is similar to those obtained in this study. Unfortunately, not enough comparable results are yet available to justify speculation on the significance of differences among the various equations.

It may be assumed, in the absence of evidence to the contrary, that the regression lines on Figures 24 to 31 represent states which can be described as normal. Given this assumption, it is interesting to examine the positions of individual centres in relation to the regression lines. Consider, for example, the relationship between populations and numbers of functions, as shown in Figures 24 and 25. On these graphs, centres lying to the left of the regression lines may be said to have a greater

[6]Brian J. L. Berry, H. Gardiner Barnum, and Robert J. Tennant, "Retail Location and Consumer Behavior," Regional Science Association, Papers and Proceedings, Vol. 9 (1962), 65-106.

TABLE 17. CONTINUOUS FUNCTIONAL RELATIONSHIPS

Independent Variable	Dependent Variable	Correlation Coefficient and Regression Equation	
		(a) Barrie System	(b) Owen Sound System
Log P	F	(a) $r = 0.870$:	$F = 30.56 \text{ Log P} - 65.79$
		(b) $r = 0.941$:	$F = 29.61 \text{ Log P} - 60.76$
F	Log E	(a) $r = 0.966$:	$\text{Log E} = 0.023\,F + 1.036$
		(b) $r = 0.986$:	$\text{Log E} = 0.023\,F + 0.981$
F	Log C	(a) $r = 0.987$:	$\text{Log C} = 0.030\,F + 1.446$
		(b) $r = 0.994$:	$\text{Log C} = 0.032\,F + 1.302$

Symbols: Log P = logarithm of population
  F = number of central functions
  Log E = logarithm of number of establishments
  Log C = logarithm of functional index

population than their number of functions would suggest, while centres to the right of the lines have more functions than is normal for their population size. A question naturally arises as to whether the residuals—that is, centres deviating widely from the regression lines—have anything in common.

Three of the residuals identified in Figures 24 and 25 can readily be rationalized as centres which would probably not exist at all if it were not for the presence of specialized non-central-place activities. First, Angus-Camp Borden, in the Barrie system, serves primarily as a dormitory for people who work either in Barrie or at the adjacent military base. These people are accustomed to shopping in Barrie for many goods, and Angus-Camp Borden itself therefore provides only a limited number of convenience functions. Secondly, Wasaga Beach and Sauble Beach are almost exclusively resort centres, and many of their functions are closed during the winter. Hence, the numbers of functions recorded for these two centres on the graphs are understandably greater than would be appropriate to serve the resident populations alone.[7]

[7]Berry has shown that it is customary for centres performing a dormitory function to have fewer central place functions than their populations suggest; see Brian J. L. Berry, "The Impact of Expanding Metropolitan Communities upon the Central Place Hierarchy," Annals of the Association of American Geographers, Vol. 50 (1960), 112-116.

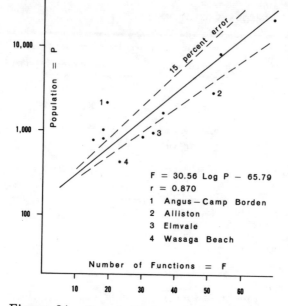
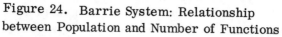

Figure 24. Barrie System: Relationship
between Population and Number of Functions

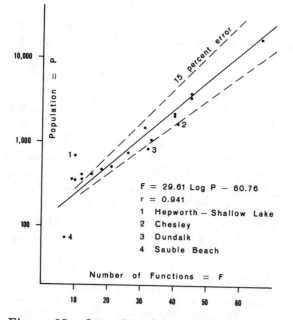

Figure 25. Owen Sound System: Relationship
between Population and Number of Functions

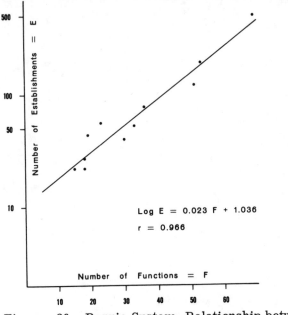

Figure. 26. Barrie System: Relationship between
Numbers of Functions and Establishments

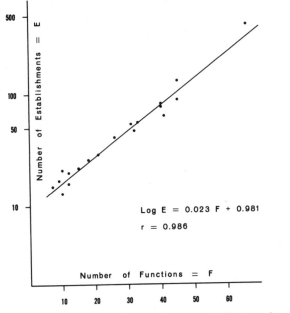

Figure 27. Owen Sound System: Relationship between
Numbers of Functions and Establishments

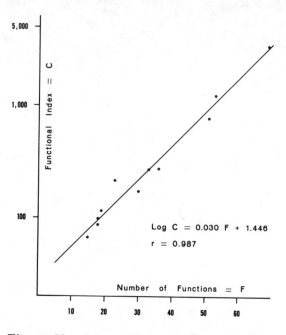

Log C = 0.030 F + 1.446

r = 0.987

Figure 28. Barrie System: Relationship
between Number of Functions and Functional Index

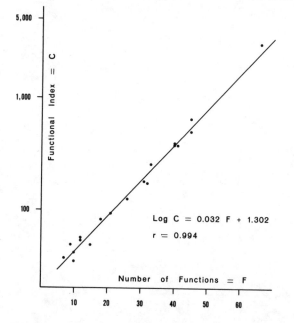

Log C = 0.032 F + 1.302

r = 0.994

Figure 29. Owen Sound System: Relationship
between Number of Functions and Functional Index

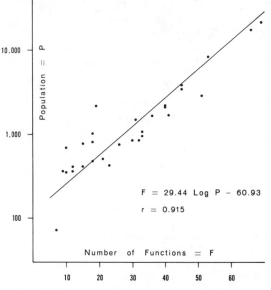

Figure 30. Barrie and Owen Sound Systems
Combined: Relationship between Population
and Number of Functions

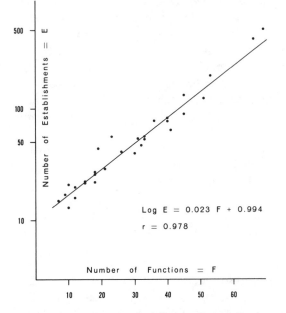

Figure 31. Barrie and Owen Sound Systems
Combined: Relationship between Numbers of
Functions and Establishments

TABLE 18. THE RELATIONSHIP BETWEEN POPULATION
AND NUMBER OF FUNCTIONS IN DIFFERENT AREAS

Study	Correlation Coefficient and Regression Equation	
Thomas[1]	$r = 0.860$:	$F = 39.91$ Log P - 66.31
Berry et al.[2]	$r = 0.953$:	$F = 50$ Log P - 105
Stafford[3]	$r = 0.892$:	$F = 24.52$ Log P - 46.43
Barrie area	$r = 0.870$:	$F = 30.56$ Log P - 65.79
Owen Sound area	$r = 0.941$:	$F = 29.61$ Log P - 60.76

Symbols: F   = number of central functions
        Log P = logarithm of population

[1]Thomas, "Some Comments on the Functional Bases for Small Iowa Towns," p. 14.

[2]Berry, Barnum, and Tennant, "Retail Location and Consumer Behavior," p. 70. In this study, the regression equation is given in the form: Log P = 0.02 F + 2.095.

[3]Stafford, "The Functional Bases of Small Towns," p. 170.

With regard to other residuals, there is a tendency for places lying to the right of the regression lines to be located relatively far from their nearest neighbours of the same or greater centrality. This is particularly true of Alliston, Elmvale, Chesley, and Dundalk. A possible explanation is that these centres, because of their greater distance from larger towns, have umlands which are larger and more populous than the norm, enabling them to provide functions which could not be sustained in a centre of equal size but with a smaller umland population.

Finally, centres lying to the left of the regression lines on Figures 24 and 25 are generally found to be close to a much larger centre in which there is some manufacturing. Examples are Cookstown (near Alliston, and not far from Barrie), Hepworth-Shallow Lake (near Owen Sound), and Elmwood (near Walkerton-Hanover). It is likely that these residuals are explained by a weakly developed dormitory function serving the nearby larger towns.

Residuals are less conspicuous on Figures 26 and 27 than on Figures 24 and 25, reflecting the fact that the number of functions in a place is a better predictor of the number of establishments there than of the place's population. The number

168

of functions is also a good predictor of a place's functional index, as shown in Figures 28 and 29. This is only to be expected, since the number of functions is itself a component of the functional index of each centre.

SUMMARY AND CONCLUSIONS

The central thesis of this study has been formed of four interlocking contentions. The first is that the concept of a central place hierarchy has an inescapable spatial component. Secondly, it is held that previous researchers, with a handful of exceptions, have ignored this spatial component. It follows, thirdly, that the growth of a coherent body of comparative generalizations about central places has been retarded. Finally, it is contended that the way out of this difficulty lies in formulating, on the basis of orthodox central place theory, a viable set of investigational techniques which can be consistently applied in empirical studies.

The argument in support of these contentions is woven around seven criteria of hierarchical structuring which are believed to be essential to the proper execution of empirical research.

Criteria of Hierarchical Structuring

The first two criteria are identified as that of the spatial interdependence of centres and that of completeness of the central place system. In effect, these criteria state that the concept of hierarchy applies only to a set of centres defined as those places which have their levels of functional development determined primarily by the level of functional complexity attained in a designated central city. This concept of a system of centres has not previously been applied in central place studies. The need for it, however, is defended on the grounds that there is no reason to expect a hierarchy to occur in the absence of some mechanism whereby towns can affect one another's functional complexity. In a properly identified system, the necessary mechanism exists by virtue of the fact that the commercial development of each centre is limited by some larger town to which it is tributary. The identification of a complete central place system has much in common with the delimitation of a

particular central city's umland, but traditional methods of umland delimitation fail to identify meaningful systems because
they do not take direct account of the intercentre linkages which
give a system its identity.

The next two criteria are those of discrete stratification of
centrality and interstitial placement of orders. These criteria
express the fact that the relative functional complexity of the
places in an ideal hierarchy is inextricably bound up with their
relative locations. The criterion of discrete stratification requires that the members of a system be grouped in such a way
that, for any two adjacent groups of centres, the between-group
difference in centrality is greater than, or at least equal to, the
within-group differences. Hand in hand with this condition goes
the criterion of interstitial placement, which states that the
members of each hierarchical order must occupy the interstices
in the pattern formed by centres of higher rank. It is conceded
that this latter criterion is by far the most difficult to translate
into objective rules for use in empirical work.

The remaining three criteria are those of incremental baskets of goods, a minimum of three orders, and a pyramidal sequence of numbers of centres in successive orders. The first
of these states that the centres in a particular hierarchical order must perform virtually all the functions found in centres in
lower orders, together with an additional group of functions not
normally performed in lower orders. The second requires that
at least three distinct orders be present in a system of centres.
The final criterion states that the number of centres in a particular order must be greater than the number in the next higher
order. The complete set of seven criteria epitomizes the fundamental characteristics of an ideal central place hierarchy.

Findings of the Study

In chapter ii, the above criteria are shown to be derived from
orthodox central place theory, the latter including Berry and
Garrison's modified version of Christaller's classical statement. Next, in chapter iii, the criteria are used as a basis
for evaluating hierarchical classifications of towns proposed
by previous investigators. With the exception of recent works
by Berry and by Skinner, past studies are found to fall well
short of verifying the existence of hierarchies of towns. In

170

particular, previous investigators have not identified meaningful systems of centres, nor have they applied the criteria of discrete stratification and interstitial placement of orders. In short, the essential spatial aspects of the hierarchy concept have been almost universally ignored. That this should be true of work carried out largely by geographers is cause for not a little dismay.

Chapter iv considers the problem of making the seven criteria operational for the purposes of empirical research. Using the whole central place as the basic unit of analysis, rather than the central function or the individual consumer, a classification of intercentre shopping linkages is devised and used as a basis for the empirical identification of central place systems. It is then argued that the centrality of the places in a properly identified central place system is well expressed by the functional index technique developed by Davies. The values of the Davies functional index for all places are combined with the topology of the Christallerian models to form a basis for the simultaneous application of the criteria of discrete stratification of centrality and interstitial placement of orders. In this way, hierarchical structuring in real central place systems may be sought with explicit recognition of the spatial aspects of the hierarchy concept. It is also proposed that the term "imperfect hierarchy" be given to a system which does not quite satisfy the criterion of discrete stratification of orders, but which can be made into a "perfect hierarchy" by arbitrary adjustment of the functional indices of not more than 20 per cent of all centres.

Finally, a case study of two adjoining central place systems in Southern Ontario is presented in an attempt to demonstrate both the validity of the seven criteria and the viability of the proposed empirical methodology. Both the Barrie and Owen Sound systems are found to be imperfect hierarchies containing four orders of centres located essentially in accordance with Christaller's Versorgungsprinzip model. In addition, the distinctive triangular lattice formed by centres of town and city rank continues unbroken throughout, and even beyond, the territory covered by the two systems, suggesting that the latter are sub-systems of some more extensive system of Ontario towns. Within the systems studied, departures from the Versorgungs-prinzip pattern appear to be satisfactorily explained by the

171

presence of non-central-place activities, by the historic importance of certain lines of transportation, and by inequalities in
the distribution of disposable income. While the two systems
are highly similar in several respects, one significant difference is that each order in the Barrie system contains functions
which are not incremental until the next higher order in the
Owen Sound system. This difference is tentatively related to
the decreasing density of rural population encountered as one
moves westwards from the Barrie system to that of Owen
Sound.

Retrospect and Prospect

Taken as a whole, this study may fairly be characterized as an
exegesis of Christaller's original approach to the study of central places. This is not to say that Christaller's work has gone
unacknowledged, for obviously it has received wide attention.
On the other hand, many writers have failed to appreciate the
spatial aspects of the hierarchy concept, and there has been a
tendency for research to proceed as if there had to be a hierarchy everywhere because that was what was "proved" by
Christaller's theory. In contrast to this attitude, Christaller
himself was well aware of the epistemological aspects of central place research. In particular, he understood the relationship between models and realities, and he recognized the need
to translate models into operational terms in order to investigate real central place networks.

Looking to the future, there appear to be two main directions which might profitably be taken by central place research.
First, there is a need for additional case studies to be carried
out using the criteria of hierarchical structuring employed in
this study. While the criteria themselves seem to be valid and
necessary, better ways may be devised of expressing them in
operational terms. In addition, it is only through the accumula-
tion of case studies that comparison of central place systems
in different parts of the world becomes possible. While the
identification of individual systems is an end in itself, comparative studies afford the prospect of still deeper insights into
the geography of central places.

Secondly, there is a great need to introduce the time dimension to central place research. What is required is not
merely the reconstruction of central place networks as they

172

existed in the past, but comparative cross-sectional studies of the same area at several different points in time. Coupled with existing central place theory, which is by nature static, such studies should lead to a deeper understanding of the evolution of central place patterns, and perhaps ultimately to the formulation of a much needed dynamic central place theory.

If this study has a paramount goal, it is to demonstrate that further progress in central place research depends upon the adoption of a unified body of empirical techniques, soundly based in theory and consistently applied to the real world. Only in this way can studies by different investigators be rendered truly comparable, and only in this way can significant generalizations about central places be established. To the extent that the need for consistency of approach is accepted, this study will have succeeded in its principal objective.

Bibliography

The literature of central place research is largely composed of short articles, and it is common for a writer to discuss the same material repetitiously in two or more publications. In the interests of clarity, the footnotes in the text refer only to each writer's most pertinent or most accessible contribution. However, a few additional works by the authors cited in the footnotes are included in this bibliography.

For convenience, materials relating to Southern Ontario and the case study area are listed in a separate section at the end of the bibliography.

For a comprehensive listing of central place studies completed up to 1964, Berry and Pred's standard bibliography may be consulted:

Berry, Brian J. L., and Pred, Allen. Central Place Studies: A Bibliography of Theory and Applications. 2nd edition. Philadelphia: Regional Science Research Institute, 1965, 152 pp. with supplement of 50 pp.

1. Central Place and Related Studies

Alexander, John W. Economic Geography. Englewood Cliffs, New Jersey: Prentice-Hall, 1963, 661 pp.

--------. "The Basic-Nonbasic Concept of Urban Economic Functions." Economic Geography, Vol. 30 (1954), 246-261.

Alexandersson, Gunnar. Geography of Manufacturing. Englewood Cliffs, New Jersey: Prentice-Hall, 1967, 154 pp.

--------. The Industrial Structure of American Cities. Lincoln: University of Nebraska Press, 1956, 134 pp.

Allix, André. "The Geography of Fairs: Illustrated by Old-World Examples." Geographical Review, Vol. 12 (1922), 532-569.

Anderson, A. H. "Space as a Social Cost." Journal of Farm Economics, Vol. 32 (1950), 411-430.

Auerbach, Felix. "Das Gesetz der Bevölkerungskonzentration." Petermanns Geographische Mitteilungen, Vol. 59, Part 1 (1913), 74-76.

Barnum, H. Gardiner. Market Centers and Hinterlands in Baden-Württemberg. Department of Geography Research Paper No. 103. Chicago: Department of Geography, University of Chicago, 1966, 173 pp.

Baskin, Carlisle W. "A Critique and Translation of Walter Christaller's Die zentralen Orte in Süddeutschland." Unpublished Ph.D. dissertation, University of Virginia, 1957.

Berry, Brian J. L. "City Size Distributions and Economic Development." Economic Development and Cultural Change, Vol. 9 (1961), 573-588.

--------. Geography of Market Centers and Retail Distribution. Englewood Cliffs, New Jersey: Prentice-Hall, 1967, 146 pp.

--------. "Grouping and Regionalizing: An Approach to the Problem Using Multivariate Analysis." Quantitative Geography: Part I: Economic and Cultural Topics. Edited by William L. Garrison and Duane F. Marble. Northwestern University Studies in Geography No. 13. Evanston, Illinois: Department of Geography, Northwestern University, 1967, pp. 219-251.

--------. "Recent Studies Concerning the Role of Transportation in the Space Economy." Annals of the Association of American Geographers, Vol. 49 (1959), 328-342.

--------. "The Impact of Expanding Metropolitan Communities upon the Central Place Hierarchy." Annals of the Association of American Geographers, Vol. 50 (1960), 112-116.

Berry, Brian J. L., and Barnum, H. Gardiner. "Aggregate Relations and Elemental Components of Central Place Systems." Journal of Regional Science, Vol. 4 (1962), 35-68.

Berry, Brian J. L., and Garrison, William L. "Alternate Explanations of Urban Rank-Size Relationships." Annals of the Association of American Geographers, Vol. 48 (1958), 83-91.

--------. "A Note on Central Place Theory and the Range of a Good." Economic Geography, Vol. 34 (1958), 304-311.

--------. "Recent Developments of Central Place Theory." Regional Science Association Papers and Proceedings, Vol. 4 (1958), 107-120.

--------. "The Functional Bases of the Central Place Hierarchy." Economic Geography, Vol. 34 (1958), 145-154.

Berry, Brian J. L., Barnum, H. Gardiner, and Tennant, Robert J. "Retail Location and Consumer Behavior." Regional Science Association, Papers and Proceedings, Vol. 9 (1962), 65-106.

Boal, F. W., and Johnson, D. B. "The Rank-Size Curve: A Diagnostic Tool?" Professional Geographer, Vol. 17, No. 5 (September, 1965), 21-23.

Borchert, John R., and Adams, Russell B. Trade Centers and Trade Areas of the Upper Midwest. Urban Report No. 3. Minneapolis: Upper Midwest Research and Development Council, 1963, 44 pp.

Bracey, Howard E. "A Rural Component of Centrality Applied to Six Southern Counties in the United Kingdom." Economic Geography, Vol. 32 (1956), 38-50.

176

--------. "English Central Villages: Identification, Distribution and Functions." Proceedings of the IGU Symposium in Urban Geography, Lund, 1960. Edited by Knut Norborg. Lund: C. W. K. Gleerup, 1962, pp. 169-190.

--------. Social Provision in Rural Wiltshire. London: Methuen, 1952, 204 pp.

--------. "Towns as Rural Service Centres." Institute of British Geographers, Transactions, No. 19 (1953), 95-105.

Brown, Robert. Explanation in Social Science. London: Routledge and Kegan Paul, 1963, 198 pp.

Brush, John E. "The Hierarchy of Central Places in Southwestern Wisconsin." Geographical Review, Vol. 43 (1953), 380-402.

Brush, John E., and Bracey, Howard E. "Rural Service Centers in Southwestern Wisconsin and Southern England." Geographical Review, Vol. 45 (1955), 559-569.

Burns, Wilfred. British Shopping Centres: New Trends in Layout and Distribution. London: L. Hill, 1959, 129 pp.

Carruthers, I. "A Classification of Service Centres in England and Wales." Geographical Journal, Vol. 123 (1957), 371-385.

Carter, Harold. The Towns of Wales: A Study in Urban Geography. Cardiff: University of Wales Press, 1965, 362 pp.

Cassady, R., and Ostlund, H. J. The Retail Distribution Structure of the Small City. University of Minnesota Studies in Economics and Business No. 12. Minneapolis: University of Minnesota, 1935, 107 pp.

Chabot, Georges. "Présentation d'une Carte des Zones d'Influence des Grandes Villes Françaises." Proceedings of the IGU Symposium in Urban Geography, Lund, 1960. Edited by Knut Norborg. Lund: C. W. K. Gleerup, 1962, pp. 197-199.

Chamberlin, Edward H. "The Product as an Economic Variable." Quarterly Journal of Economics, Vol. 67 (1953), 1-29.

Chatelain, Abel. "Géographie Sociologique de la Presse et Régions Françaises." Revue de Géographie de Lyon, Vol. 32 (1957), 127-134.

Chilczuk, M. "Functions and Dynamics of Transitional Type Settlements in Poland." Geographia Polonica, Vol. 2 (1964), 133-138.

Christaller, Walter. Central Places in Southern Germany. Translated by Carlisle W. Baskin. Englewood Cliffs, New Jersey: Prentice-Hall, 1966, 230 pp.

Clark, Colin. "The Economic Functions of a City in Relation to Its Size." Econometrica, Vol. 13 (1945), 97-113.

Clark, Philip J., and Evans, Francis C. "Distance to Nearest Neighbor as a Measure of Spatial Relationships in Populations." Ecology, Vol. 35 (1954), 445-453.

Condon, E. U. "Statistics of Vocabulary." Science, Vol. 67 (1928), 300.

Constandse, A. K. "Reclamation and Colonisation of New Areas." Tijdschrift voor Economische en Sociale Geografie, Vol. 54 (1963), 41-45.

177

Coppolani, Jean. Le Réseau Urbain de la France: Sa Structure et Son Aménagement. Paris: Editions Ouvrières, 1959, 80 pp.

Davies, Wayne K. D. "Centrality and the Central Place Hierarchy." Urban Studies, Vol. 4 (1967), 61-79.

--------. "Some Considerations of Scale in Central Place Analysis." Tijdschrift voor Economische en Sociale Geografie, Vol. 56 (1965), 221-227.

--------. "The Ranking of Service Centres: A Critical Review." Institute of British Geographers, Transactions, No. 40 (1966), 51-65.

Deasy, G. F. "Sales and Service Industries in Luce County, Michigan." Economic Geography, Vol. 26 (1950), 315-324.

Dickinson, Robert E. City Region and Regionalism. London: Routledge and Kegan Paul, 1947, 327 pp.

--------. "The Distribution and Functions of the Smaller Urban Settlements of East Anglia." Geography, Vol. 17 (1932), 19-31.

--------. "The Regional Functions and Zones of Influence of Leeds and Bradford." Geography, Vol. 15 (1929-30), 548-557.

Duncan, J. S. "New Zealand Towns as Service Centres." New Zealand Geographer, Vol. 11 (1955), 119-138.

Duncan, Otis D. "Service Industries and the Urban Hierarchy." Regional Science Association, Papers and Proceedings, Vol. 5 (1959), 105-120.

--------. "Urbanization and Retail Specialization." Social Forces, Vol. 30 (1952), 267-271.

Duncan, Otis D., Scott, William R., Lieberson, Stanley, Duncan, Beverly D., and Winsborough, Hal H. Metropolis and Region. Baltimore: Johns Hopkins Press, 1960, 587 pp.

Fleming, J. B. "An Analysis of Shops and Service Trades in Scottish Towns." Scottish Geographical Magazine, Vol. 70 (1954), 97-106.

Florence, P. S. "Economic Efficiency in the Metropolis." The Metropolis in Modern Life. Edited by Robert M. Fisher. New York: Doubleday, 1955, pp. 85-124.

Fuguitt, Glenn V., and Deeley, Nora A. "Retail Service Patterns and Small Town Population Change: A Replication of Hassinger's Study." Rural Sociology, Vol. 31 (1966), 53-63.

Fullerton, B. The Pattern of Service Industries in Northeast England. Department of Geography Research Series No. 3. Newcastle upon Tyne: Department of Geography, King's College, University of Durham, 1960, 43 pp.

Galpin, Charles J. The Social Anatomy of an Agricultural Community. Research Bulletin No. 34. Madison: University of Wisconsin Agricultural Experiment Station, 1915, 34 pp.

Gauchy, Marcel. "Le Rayonnement des Journaux Toulousains." Revue Géographique des Pyrénées et du Sud-Ouest, Vol. 26 (1955), 100-112.

Getis, Arthur, and Getis, Judith. "Christaller's Central Place Theory." Journal of Geography, Vol. 65 (1966), 220-226.

Godlund, Sven. "Bus Services, Hinterlands, and the Location of Urban Settlements in Sweden, Specially in Scania." Lund Studies in Geography, Series B, No. 3 (1951), 14-24.

Golachowski, Stefan. "Rola Teorii Christallera w Planowaniu Hitlerowskim na Slasku." Studia Slaskie, No. 10 (1964), 167-177.

Green, F. H. W. "Bus Services in the British Isles." Geographical Review, Vol. 41 (1951), 645-655.

--------. "Community of Interest and Local Government Areas." Public Administration, Vol. 34 (1956), 39-49.

--------. "Community of Interest Areas: Notes on the Hierarchy of Central Places and Their Hinterlands." Economic Geography, Vol. 34 (1958), 210-226.

--------. "Urban Hinterlands in England and Wales: An Analysis of Bus Services." Geographical Journal, Vol. 116 (1950), 64-81.

Grove, David, and Huszar, Laszlo. The Towns of Ghana: The Role of Service Centres in Regional Planning. Accra: Ghana Universities Press, 1964, 98 pp.

Haggett, P., and Gunawardena, K. A. "Determination of Population Thresholds for Settlement Functions by the Reed-Muench Method." Professional Geographer, Vol. 16, No. 4 (July, 1964), 6-9.

Harris, Chauncy D. "City and Region in the Soviet Union." Urbanization and Its Problems. Edited by R. P. Beckinsale and J. M. Houston. Oxford: Basil Blackwell, 1968, pp. 277-296.

Harris, Chauncy D., and Ullman, Edward L. "The Nature of Cities." Annals of the American Academy of Political and Social Science, Vol. 242 (1945), 7-17.

Hassinger, Edward. "The Relationship of Retail-Service Patterns to Trade-Center Population Change." Rural Sociology, Vol. 22 (1957), 235-240.

Haughton, J. P. "Local Newspapers and the Regional Geographer." Advancement of Science, Vol. 7 (1950), 44-45.

Hoffer, Charles R. "The Changing Ecological Pattern in Rural Life." Rural Sociology, Vol. 13 (1948), 176-180.

Houston, James M. A Social Geography of Europe. London: Duckworth, 1953, 271 pp.

Iowa. A Retail Trading Area Analysis of Jefferson, Iowa. Iowa City: Bureau of Business and Economic Research, University of Iowa, 1965, 182 pp.

Isard, Walter. Location and Space-Economy. Cambridge: Massachusetts Institute of Technology Press, 1956, 350 pp.

Jefferson, Mark. "Distribution of the World's City Folks." Geographical Review, Vol. 21 (1931), 446-465.

Johnson, James H. Urban Geography: An Introductory Analysis. Oxford: Pergamon Press, 1967, 188 pp.

Johnston, R. J. "The Measurement of a Hierarchy of Central Places." Australian Geographer, Vol. 9 (1964-65), 315-317.

Kaniowna, Czeslawa. "Problem Osiedli Centralnych w Bylej Rejencji Opolskiej." Materialy i Studia Opolskie, No. 4 (1963), 95-99.

Kar, N. R. "Urban Hierarchy and Central Functions around Calcutta in Lower West Bengal, India, and Their Significance." Proceedings of the IGU Symposium in Urban Geography, Lund, 1960. Edited by Knut Norborg. Lund: C. W. K. Gleerup, 1962, pp. 253-274.

Keeble, Lewis. Principles and Practice of Town and Country Planning. 2nd edition. London: Estates Gazette, 1959, 338 pp.

Kendall, H. M. "Fairs and Markets in the Department of Gers, France." Economic Geography, Vol. 12 (1936), 351-358.

Kielczewska-Zaleska, Maria. "Geographical Studies on Rural Settlement in Poland." Geographia Polonica, Vol. 1 (1964), 97-110.

King, Leslie J. "The Functional Role of Small Towns in Canterbury." Proceedings of the Third New Zealand Geography Conference. Palmerston North: New Zealand Geographical Society, 1961, pp. 139-149.

Kolb, John H. Emerging Rural Communities. Madison: University of Wisconsin Press, 1959, 212 pp.

--------. Service Relations of Town and Country. Research Bulletin No. 58. Madison: University of Wisconsin Agricultural Experiment Station, 1923, 78 pp.

Kosinski, Leszek. "Population and Urban Geography in Poland." Geographia Polonica, Vol. 1 (1964), 79-96.

Lipman, V. D. "Town and Country: The Study of Service Centres and Their Areas of Influence." Public Administration, Vol. 30 (1952), 203-214.

Lösch, August. The Economics of Location. Translated by William H. Woglom and Wolfgang F. Stolper. New Haven: Yale University Press, 1954, 520 pp.

--------. "The Nature of Economic Regions." Southern Economic Journal, Vol. 5 (1938), 71-78.

Lomas, G. M. "Retail Trading Centres in the Midlands." Journal of the Town Planning Institute, Vol. 50 (1964), 104-119.

Lotka, Alfred J. "The Frequency Distribution of Scientific Productivity." Journal of the Washington Academy of Sciences, Vol. 16 (1926), 317-323.

Lukermann, Frederick. "Empirical Expressions of Nodality and Hierarchy in a Circulation Manifold." East Lakes Geographer, Vol. 2 (1966), 17-44.

Mayer, Harold M. "A Survey of Urban Geography." The Study of Urbanization. Edited by Philip M. Hauser and Leo F. Schnore. New York: Wiley, 1965, pp. 81-113.

Mayfield, Robert C. "A Central-Place Hierarchy in Northern India." Quantitative Geography: Part I: Economic and Cultural Topics. Edited by William L. Garrison and Duane F. Marble. Northwestern University Studies in Geography No. 13. Evanston, Illinois: Department of Geography, Northwestern University, 1967, pp. 120-166.

--------. "The Range of a Central Good in the Indian Punjab." Annals of the Association of American Geographers, Vol. 53 (1963), 38–49.

Melvin, Ernest E. "Native Urbanism in West Africa." Journal of Geography, Vol. 60 (1961), 9–16.

Moore, Frederick T. "A Note on City Size Distributions." Economic Development and Cultural Change, Vol. 7 (1958–59), 465–466.

Morrill, Richard L. "Simulation of Central Place Patterns over Time." Proceedings of the IGU Symposium in Urban Geography, Lund, 1960. Edited by Knut Norborg. Lund: C. W. K. Gleerup, 1962, pp. 109–120.

Murphy, Raymond E. The American City: An Urban Geography. New York: McGraw-Hill, 1966, 464 pp.

Nystuen, John D., and Dacey, Michael F. "A Graph Theory Interpretation of Nodal Regions." Regional Science Association, Papers and Proceedings, Vol. 7 (1961), 29–42.

Palomäki, Mauri. "The Functional Centers and Areas of South Bothnia, Finland." Fennia, Vol. 88, No. 1 (1964), 1–235.

Park, Robert E. "Urbanization as Measured by Newspaper Circulation." American Journal of Sociology, Vol. 35 (1929), 60–79.

Park, Robert E., and Newcomb, Charles. "Newspaper Circulation and Metropolitan Regions." Contributed in Roderick D. McKenzie, The Metropolitan Community. New York: McGraw-Hill, 1933, pp. 98–110.

Passmore, J. "Explanation in Everyday Life, in Science, and in History." History and Theory, Vol. 2 (1962), 105–123.

Reed, L. J., and Muench, H. "A Simple Method of Estimating Fifty Per Cent Endpoints." American Journal of Hygiene, Vol. 27 (1938), 493–497.

Reilly, William J. Methods for the Study of Retail Relationships. Studies in Marketing No. 4. Austin: Bureau of Business Research, University of Texas, 1959, 50 pp. A reprint of the 1929 edition.

--------. The Law of Retail Gravitation. New York: By the author, 1931.

Rosing, Kenneth E. "A Rejection of the Zipf Model (Rank Size Rule) in Relation to City Size." Professional Geographer, Vol. 18, No. 2 (March, 1966), 75–82.

Saskatchewan. Royal Commission on Agriculture and Rural Life. Report No. 12. Service Centers. Regina: Queen's Printer, 1957, 154 pp.

Schettler, C. "Relation of City-Size to Economic Services." American Sociological Review, Vol. 8 (1943), 60–62.

Schwartz, George. "Laws of Retail Gravitation: An Appraisal." University of Washington Business Review, Vol. 22, No. 1 (October, 1962), 53–70.

Scott, Peter. "Areal Variations in the Class Structure of the Central-Place Hierarchy." Australian Geographical Studies, Vol. 2 (1964), 73–86.

--------. "The Hierarchy of Central Places in Tasmania." Australian Geographer, Vol. 9 (1964–65), 134–147.

181

--------. "The Measurement of a Hierarchy of Central Places: A Reply." Australian
Geographer, Vol. 9 (1964-65), 317-318.

Singer, H. W. "The 'Courbe des Populations': A Parallel to Pareto's Law." Economic
Journal, Vol. 46 (1936), 254-263.

Skinner, G. William. "Marketing and Social Structure in Rural China: Part I." Journal
of Asian Studies, Vol. 24 (1964-65), 3-43.

--------. "Marketing and Social Structure in Rural China: Part II." Journal of Asian
Studies, Vol. 24 (1964-65), 195-228.

--------. "Marketing and Social Structure in Rural China: Part III." Journal of Asian
Studies, Vol. 24 (1964-65), 363-399.

Smailes, Arthur E. "The Analysis and Delimitation of Urban Fields." Geography, Vol.
32 (1947), 151-161.

--------. "The Urban Hierarchy in England and Wales." Geography, Vol. 29 (1944),
41-51.

--------. "Town and Region." Planning Outlook, Vol. 2, No. 2 (1951), 16-26.

Smith, Robert H. T. "Method and Purpose in Functional Town Classification." Annals
of the Association of American Geographers, Vol. 55 (1965), 539-548.

Snyder, David E. "Urban Places in Uruguay and the Concept of a Hierarchy." Festschrift
Clarence F. Jones. Edited by Merle C. Prunty. Northwestern University Studies in
Geography No. 6. Evanston, Illinois: Department of Geography, Northwestern Univer
sity, 1962, pp. 29-46.

Stafford, Howard A. "The Functional Bases of Small Towns." Economic Geography, Vol.
39 (1963), 165-175.

Stewart, Charles T. "The Size and Spacing of Cities." Geographical Review, Vol. 48
(1958), 222-245.

Stewart, John Q. "A Basis for Social Physics." Impact of Science on Society, Vol. 3
(1952), 110-133.

Stine, James H. "Temporal Aspects of Tertiary Production Elements in Korea." Urban
Systems and Economic Development. Edited by Forrest R. Pitts. Eugene: School
of Business Administration, University of Oregon, 1962, pp. 68-88.

Stoll, Walter D. "Characteristics of Shopping Centers." Traffic Quarterly, Vol. 21
(1967), 159-177.

Strohkarck, Frank, and Phelps, Katherine. "The Mechanics of Constructing a Market
Area Map." Journal of Marketing, Vol. 12 (1947-48), 493-496.

Takes, C. A. P. "The Settlement Pattern in the Dutch Zuiderzee Reclamation Scheme."
Tijdschrift van het Koninklijk Nederlandsch Aardrijkskundig Genootschap, Vol. 77
(1960), 347-353.

Tatarkiewicz, Wladyslaw. "Nomological and Typological Sciences." Journal of Philosophy, Vol. 57 (1960), 234-240.

Thoman, Richard S., and Yeates, Maurice H. Delimitation of Development Regions in Canada (With Special Attention to the Georgian Bay Vicinity). Ottawa: Area Development Agency, Department of Industry, 1966, 134 pp.

Thomas, Edwin N. "Some Comments on the Functional Bases for Small Iowa Towns." Iowa Business Digest, Vol. 31, No. 2 (February, 1960), 10-16.

Thorndike, E. L. Review of George K. Zipf, National Unity and Disunity: The Nation as a Bio-Social Organism. Science, Vol. 94 (1941), 19.

Trotier, Louis. "Some Functional Characteristics of the Main Service Centres of the Province of Quebec." Cahiers de Géographie de Québec, No. 6 (1959), 243-259.

Ullman, Edward L. "A Theory of Location for Cities." American Journal of Sociology, Vol. 46 (1941), 853-864.

--------. "Trade Centers and Tributary Areas of the Philippines." Geographical Review, Vol. 50 (1960), 203-218.

Vining, Rutledge. "A Description of Certain Spatial Aspects of an Economic System." Economic Development and Cultural Change, Vol. 3 (1954-55), 147-195.

Wade, Richard C. The Urban Frontier. Cambridge: Harvard University Press, 1959, 360 pp.

Watkins, J. W. N. "Ideal Types and Historical Explanation." British Journal for the Philosophy of Science, Vol. 3 (1952-53), 22-43.

Woroby, P. "Functional Ranks and Locational Patterns of Service Centres in Saskatchewan" (abstract). Canadian Geographer, No. 14 (1959), 43.

Zipf, George K. Human Behavior and the Principle of Least Effort. Cambridge: Addison-Wesley Press, 1949, 573 pp.

--------. National Unity and Disunity: The Nation as a Bio-Social Organism. Bloomington, Indiana: Principia Press, 1941, 408 pp.

2. Case Study Materials

Bank Directory of Canada. July, 1966. Toronto: Houstons Standard Publications.

Brewers Retail Store Directory, 1966-67. Toronto: Brewers Warehousing Company.

Canada. Dominion Bureau of Statistics. 1961 Census of Canada. Several volumes. Ottawa: Queen's Printer, various dates.

Canada. Postmaster General. List of Post Offices with Revenues for the Year Ended March 31, 1961. Ottawa: Queen's Printer, 1961.

Canadian Advertising Rates and Data. August, 1967. Toronto: Maclean-Hunter.

Canadian Almanac and Directory for 1967. Toronto: Copp Clark.

Canadian Hospital Directory, 1966. Toronto: Canadian Hospital Association.

Canadian Medical Directory, 1967. Toronto: Current Publications.

183

Chapman, L. J., and Putnam, D. F. The Physiography of Southern Ontario. 2nd edition. Toronto: University of Toronto Press, 1966, 386 pp.

Dun and Bradstreet of Canada Limited. Reference Book: November, 1965. Toronto: Dun and Bradstreet.

LCBO Price List. May, 1966. Toronto: Liquor Control Board of Ontario.

Merriam, Willis B. "Reclamation Economy in the Holland Marsh Area of Ontario." Journal of Geography, Vol. 60 (1961), 135-140.

Ontario. Department of Archives. Sixteenth Report. Land Settlement in Upper Canada, 1783-1840, by Gilbert C. Paterson. Toronto: King's Printer, 1921, 278 pp.

Ontario. Department of Economics and Development. Georgian Bay Region: Economic Survey. Toronto: Ontario Department of Economics and Development, 1963, 132 pp.

--------. Industrial Directory of Municipal Data. 2 volumes. Toronto: Ontario Department of Economics and Development, 1967.

Ontario. Department of Municipal Affairs. 1967 Municipal Directory. Toronto: Ontario Department of Municipal Affairs.